SPOOKY
Maryland

SPOOKY
Maryland

Tales of Hauntings, Strange Happenings, and Other Local Lore

SECOND EDITION

RETOLD BY S. E. SCHLOSSER
ILLUSTRATED BY PAUL G. HOFFMAN

Globe Pequot
GUILFORD, CONNECTICUT

Globe
Pequot

An imprint of The Rowman & Littlefield Publishing Group, Inc.
4501 Forbes Blvd., Ste. 200
Lanham, MD 20706
www.rowman.com

Distributed by NATIONAL BOOK NETWORK

British Library Cataloguing in Publication Information available

Library of Congress Cataloging-in-Publication Data available

ISBN 978-1-4930-4479-5 (paper)
ISBN 978-1-4930-4480-1 (electronic)

Contents

Contents

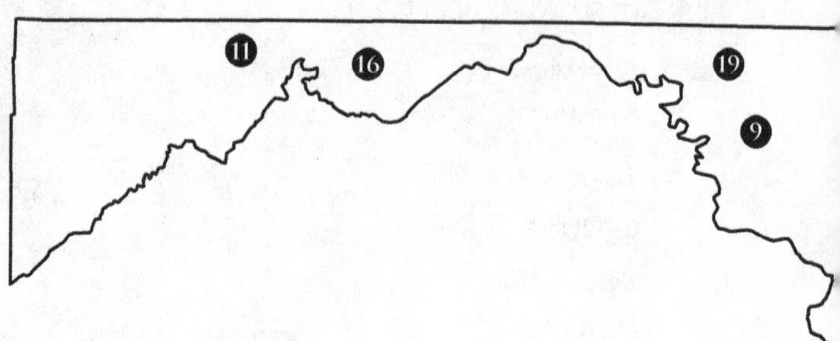

1. Salisbury
2. Bethesda
3. Annapolis
4. Crisfield
5. Venton
6. Cambridge
7. Ocean City
8. Baltimore
9. Boonsboro
10. Dorchester County
11. Frostburg
12. Baltimore
13. Clinton
14. Berlin
15. Calvert County
16. Allegany County
17. Bowie
18. Cambridge
19. Hagerstown
20. Baltimore
21. Smith Island
22. Upper Malboro
23. Somerset County
24. Ward's Crossing
25. Baltimore
26. Ellicot City
27. Worchester County
28. St. Marys County
29. Pikesville
30. Hoopers Island
31. Easton
32. St. Charles
33. Baltimore
34. Prince George's County

29
12
8
20
26
25
33
2
34
17
3
22
13
24
31
6
18
32
15
10
1
14
7
30
5
27
23
28
21
4

Introduction

I swung my overnight bag out of the trunk of the car, already relaxing as I breathed in the salty air of the quiet waterfront fishing village of Solomons Island, where the Patuxent River meets the Chesapeake Bay. The garden beside the Victorian guesthouse where I'd booked a room for the night was nicely shaded, and on the far side of the road I could see water sparkling in the golden light of a summer's afternoon. After noisy, crowded Washington, D.C. (where I'd spent the last few hours marching around the National Mall with my family, arguing amiably with my sister, and making sure that my nieces and nephews didn't fall, run into someone, get lost, or drown themselves in an ornamental pool), this was sheer heaven!

I unpacked as fast as I could, eager to explore, and quickly made my way out to the street. I slowed down immediately upon exiting the guesthouse, for such a lovely afternoon in such a place surely shouldn't be rushed. I admired the sailboats in the marina as I meandered down the sidewalk, prior to eyeing a very large, completely out-of-place tiki bar that was already starting to bustle with activity. It was obviously a haunt of the locals, though I was taken aback to find it on a Chesapeake Bay island rather than a tropical one in the Caribbean.

I was aiming for the boardwalk, where I could hear a live band playing. Feeling the cool breeze coming off the water as I rounded a corner, I gave a sigh of contentment. This was the life!

I quickly located the restaurant recommended by the guesthouse manager and ordered a delicious dinner. I declined dessert, though, my thoughts drifting back to a certain ice-cream stand I'd passed on the boardwalk. As I strolled toward my chosen dessert, I contemplated the various ghost stories I had managed to worm out of the waitstaff at the restaurant. A haunted lighthouse, a mysterious state park, and a ghost ship were all mentioned in the course of my meal. There was, however, no hint of the story that had brought me down to Calvert County in the first place. It was an intriguing folktale—more than a hundred years old—in which an elder brother altered a will in his favor, virtually disowning his two brothers in the process, until his father's ghost interceded on their behalf (*Handprint*).

Of course, researching an old folktale was not the only reason I had come to Solomons Island that fine summer day. I also intended to visit the Calvert Marine Museum, where I hoped to gain insight into what it meant to be a Chesapeake Bay waterman. I found the folklore of the watermen rich and varied and quite delightful. Their sense of humor was as salty as the Bay, and their tales of hauntings and witches and spooky creatures would keep even the most stouthearted person awake late into the night, with every light in the house turned on into the bargain!

On one end of the spectrum, I found myself haunted by the story of a man's fatal encounter with a certain will-o'-the-wisp, a bitter creature who lures the unwary to their death in the swamplands with his light (*Jack O'Lantern*). On the other, I couldn't stop laughing over the story of a waterman who stole a corpse's jacket and was plagued by his ghost until he returned it (*Dead Man's Coat*). Then there was the young waterman-turned-soldier who survived the Battle of Antietam, only to find the ghost of his best friend haunting him when he returned safely home to Annapolis (*The Headless Confederate*).

From the summer residents of Ocean City to the coal miners and farmers of the Appalachian Mountains in the west, Maryland is a state of endless variety and endless folklore. Yet beneath the surface of this state full of contrasts, I found the underlying story themes to be oddly similar, as if the people of Maryland were united, even though the topography of the land and the professions of her citizens living therein were disparate. The statue of Black Aggie once terrorized an entire generation of people in Pikesville, while Crooked Kate the witch did the same for watermen along the Eastern Shore. A waterman on Smith Island once found a pirate chest full of gold (*Marmaduke Mister's Gold*), while a housewife in Frostburg was directed to several jars full of money by the spirit of an old miser (*The Ghost in the Chimney*). And the Devil . . . that wily old soul . . . plays a few rounds of poker at Ward's Crossing on the Eastern Shore (*The Card Game*) after playing another, much more deadly game in Baltimore (*The Devil's Racecourse*).

From the ice-creamy first day of my visit to Maryland to my sunburnt, beach-filled last, I enjoyed every minute of my time in this state. I spoke to watermen, soldiers, housewives, museum workers, day-trippers, businessmen, store owners, and many, many other people who make Maryland their home. This book is for all of them.

—Sandy Schlosser

PART ONE
Ghost Stories

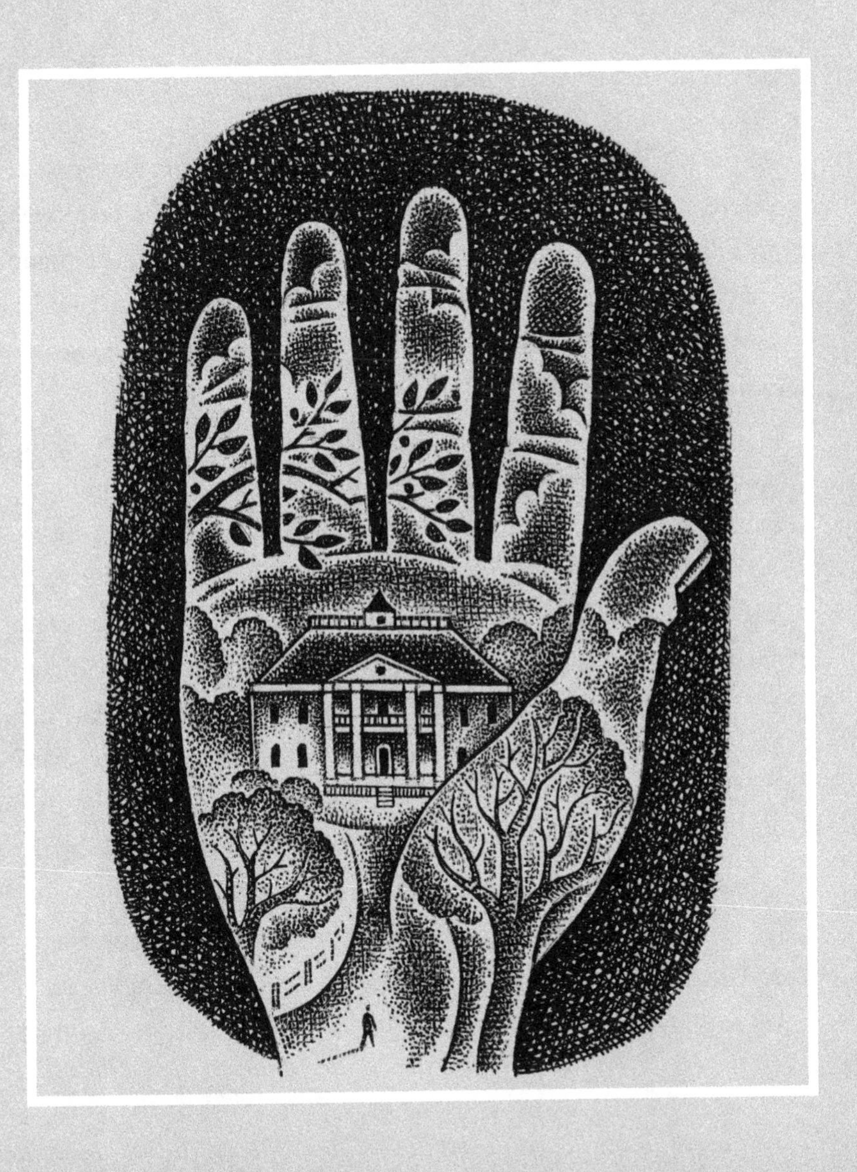

1

Whalem-Balem

SALISBURY

There's a story I heard once about a preacher-man who was offered a lot of money if he stayed all night in a house to prove to folks it wasn't haunted. The preacher didn't have more than two pennies to his name on account of his preaching job didn't pay too well, so he agreed to spend a whole night in the creepy old house.

Well, the preacher took his Bible and some food with him, since there was no reason to starve himself while he was waiting for the haunts to appear. When he got there, he walked right up the rotten old porch and through the creaking door into a wide entrance hall liberally strewn with long, dusty cobwebs. He glanced at his reflection in a large, cracked mirror with an ornate gold frame and straightened his cap. In the mirror, he caught a glimpse of another room opening off the entrance hall full of sheet-covered furniture. In the dimness of twilight, the sheets looked like ghosts, and the preacher gave a muffled shriek of alarm before realizing what they were.

The preacher was mighty glad there wasn't anyone there to hear his silly yell. To prove to himself that he wasn't scared of any haunts, he walked through all the downstairs rooms, looking in shadowy corners and at shrouded furniture and empty bookshelves and dead fireplaces. Then he marched through the narrow passage over creaking floorboards until he found a large kitchen in the back. It had dusty counters and blackened pots and pans hanging around a huge empty fireplace. Sounds echoed strangely off the walls, as if the preacher were sitting in a cavern instead of a house, and the cobwebs hung so low that he had to grab a broom and clear them away before he could reach the fireplace.

There was a pile of rotting wood in a box beside the hearth, and the preacher knelt in front of the dirty old grate and made himself a big, hot fire. The bright light and colorful flames cheered him up after his trek through the spooky old house. The preacher set his meat and potatoes to sizzling in a big frying pan and then sat on a ragged old couch next to the fireplace and started reading his Bible.

About that time, a cool, damp breeze came whirling through the kitchen, ruffling the preacher's hair and making him shiver with cold. It was a clear, warm, moonlit night, but the cool breeze smelled of decaying leaves and rain. The heat of the fire and its friendly crackling became muted as the chill wind whipped around him.

Then the preacher heard a drip, drip, dripping sound from the far side of the kitchen, near the sink with the pump beside it. He gripped the edges of his Bible tightly. No one had used the pump in years, so it shouldn't be dripping. Then a ball of light appeared, illuminating the shadowy sink and slowly transforming into the blue, choking face of a drowned man, his long hair rippling and streaming like seaweed around his twisted countenance.

"Preacher," the drowned head wheezed. "Are you gonna stay here 'til Whalem-Balem comes?"

The preacher shivered and shook next to the hot fire and didn't say a word. Slowly, the drowned man's head faded away, and the ghostly breeze along with it. The crackling of the fire was suddenly loud again in the preacher's ears, and once more he felt the warmth of the flames and smelled the enticing scent of frying meat and potatoes.

Well, that ghost wasn't scary, thought the preacher, forgetting his fright now that the kitchen had gone back to normal. All the same, he wondered who or what this Whalem-Balem might be of which the drowned head had spoken.

The preacher leaned forward to stir his meat and potatoes in the snapping, sizzling skillet. As he did, a blast of frigid air smelling of manure and the barnyard nearly knocked him off the battered old couch. Once again the ghostly breeze muted the crackle and warmth of the fire. The preacher dropped the spoon onto the hearth and whirled around. Stamping a hoof impatiently on the tiled floor beside the back door was the glowing, headless body of a mule. It shook itself all over, and then the body winked out of existence and the mule's pop-eyed head materialized in its place, floating a few feet above the floor.

"Preacher-man," the mule brayed. "Are you gonna stay here 'til Whalem-Balem comes?"

The preacher shivered and shook next to the hot fire and didn't say a word. Slowly, the mule's head faded away, and the frigid breeze disappeared. The crackling sound of the fire returned, and the preacher felt the warmth of the flames and once again smelled the cooking meat and potatoes. The preacher was nonplussed at the appearance of a second ghost.

WHALEM-BALEM

He grabbed his Bible and held it tight. Maybe this job wasn't so easy after all. And who was Whalem-Balem?

Then he smelled burning meat and realized that his supper would be ruined if he didn't tend to it right-quick. Retrieving the spoon from the floor of the hearth, he bent over the skillet and gave everything a good stir. Behind him, the air began to swirl around and around, getting colder and colder as the smell of dusty hay filled the room, dampening the warmth of the fire and the cheery crackling of the flames. The preacher carefully finished stirring his supper, which he could no longer smell, and then turned to face the third haunt.

An extremely large black cat with red eyes was lying lazily on top of a glowing bale of hay, and the kitchen around it was overlaid with a sketchy, quivering picture of the hayloft where the cat had once lived. The black cat rose and stretched its enormous body front and then back. Then it padded right up to the preacher, blinked its fiery eyes and meowed: "Preacher-man, do you really think it wise to stay here 'til Whalem-Balem comes?"

The preacher stared mutely into the creature's red eyes, shivering and shaking, until it vanished, taking the whirling wind away with it. The happy crackling of the fire returned, and the preacher felt the warmth of the flames and smelled the meat and potatoes yet again.

But this time the fire failed to warm his shaking body, and deep inside he wondered what he should do. Should he wait here until Whalem-Balem came? He needed the money, but did he need it this much?

With shaking hands, he used the spoon to lift the meat and potatoes onto his tin plate. As he did, the back door burst open under the force of a frigid wind, and a flaming creature with the body of a dog, the tusks of a boar, and the evil eyes of a demon rushed into the room. The preacher dropped his plate on the floor, and the creature downed its contents in one large gulp. Then it lifted wicked eyes to the cowering preacher and roared: "Preacher-man, are you gonna stay here 'til Whalem-Balem comes?"

"No, I ain't!" the preacher roared back at the creature, and he lit out of the open door faster than a cottontail with a coyote after it.

The preacher wouldn't go near that house again, not even to fetch his abandoned Bible. He just packed up his meager belongings and moved right out of the state to get as far away from Whalem-Balem and the haunted house as he could.

2

Cruel Master

BETHESDA

Once upon a dark time, long before Mr. Lincoln freed the slaves, there was a cruel master who had not one spark of decency in him. He whipped his slaves until they were senseless, sold his own children away from their mothers, and beat his wife if she interfered on anyone's behalf. The slaves hated him passionately, and a few tried to run away. When they were caught, he had them severely punished. Many slaves died under this cruel master.

One day the master woke in a foul temper—even fouler than usual, that is. On a whim, he grabbed the first slave he encountered, a frail elderly woman. He stripped off her clothes and tied her wrists to the branches of a tree. All day long, whenever he passed the tree, he would whip her across her bare back until she screamed in agony.

Hour after hour, the unoffending old woman stood in the chilly rain, blood dripping down her back. When some of the younger slaves went to her, she begged them to leave so that they would not suffer a similar fate.

The cruel master drank heavily at dinner and staggered away from the dining table to sit by the fire. His wife, deciding that her husband was too drunk to leave the house, crept out to the tree where the old woman sagged in agony. She cut the poor slave down and helped her home, treated her wounds, and gave her a soothing herbal drink to ease her pain.

When the wife returned to the house, she was met by her cruel husband, who had just discovered what she had done. He struck his wife across the face so hard that she fell senseless to the floor. Then he stormed out of the house and made his way to the stable. He kicked the stable boy awake, and the lad staggered dazedly into the stall to saddle his master's horse.

Back at the house, a lovely, middle-aged slave tenderly gathered up her mistress and carried her to the bedroom. Then she took a spare sheet from the closet and fled out into the dark, drizzling night. It was her mother who had suffered under the cruel master's whip that day, and she was determined to have her revenge.

The one thing the cruel master feared was ghosts, and so the lovely slave-woman ran out to the lane and hid behind a gnarled tree to wait for the master to ride past. After a few tense minutes, she heard the thunder of hooves. Flinging the sheet over her head, she gave a hideous shriek and leapt out into the center of the lane. The horse shied in fright and the cruel master gave a scream of terror. The horse dodged the white figure and fled, slamming heavily against the old gnarled tree behind which the slave-woman had hidden herself. Master and horse crashed to the ground, which trembled from the weight of their fall. The slave-woman did not stop to check on their well-being. She was back beside her mistress's unconscious body within ten minutes, the sheet tucked in with the other soiled linen.

The cruel master and his horse were discovered by a workman the next morning—both dead from injuries caused by

CRUEL MASTER

the collision with the tree. Their blood stained the trunk of the tree for many days. Underneath the bloodstains, the shattered images of the cruel master and his horse slowly took form, burned into the bark by the hot blood of the slave-woman's victims. For many months following the accident, the sound of the cruel master's scream and the terrible, final crash as he and his horse slammed into the tree would echo through the night air whenever it rained. Sometimes, the slaves would gather in the lane to listen to the ghostly noises. But not one of them ever shed a tear for their departed master.

3

The Headless Confederate

ANNAPOLIS

Billy and Charlie were unlikely pals, what with Billy being the son of an oysterman and Charlie the son of the local blacksmith. Land and sea, they called themselves, and stuck together through thick and thin, getting into scrapes and wheedling their way back out, having a bit of schooling when their fathers could spare them from the family business, and generally bossing all the other boys in the neighborhood around. Stephan, the carpenter's son, sometimes made up the third member of their gang, when the boys' activities weren't too strenuous. Stephan was lame in one leg and deemed too delicate to do any heavy carpentry. But he could carve like a dream and was already earning some money for his specialized handiwork.

Stephan's little sister, Lucy, started tagging along after the boys from the moment she could walk. She absolutely adored Billy and would spend all day on the docks of Annapolis, waiting for his father's Bugeye sailboat to come in with the day's catch. They'd walk home together, Billy smelling of oysters and salty air, and Lucy smelling of the flowers she always picked along the side of the road. It was generally understood among the three boys that Billy was going to marry Lucy someday.

When Billy was sixteen, his uncle offered him a place on his merchant ship. After talking it over with his folks, Billy decided it was a good opportunity. He would earn enough in one voyage to buy his own Bugeye and a small house. So he bade his family farewell, kissed Lucy for the very first time on the dock next to the merchant ship, and went to sea.

The voyage was rough from the start. After several grueling months trading in the Caribbean, an early-season typhoon ripped apart the ship, leaving Billy stranded on a small island for months. When at last he made it home, two years after his departure, he found his mother dead from pneumonia and Lucy married to his best buddy—Charlie.

Lucy's father had died the year before. Following his demise, the family had learned that he was a reckless gambler who had left them with a string of debts and no money. Their house was sold to pay off some of the lenders, and Stephan used the money he had saved from carving to appease the rest. But the family was penniless and had nowhere to turn. Charlie had stepped in and offered them a home, with the tacit understanding that Lucy's hand in marriage would seal the deal. Believing Billy lost at sea, the grieving girl agreed to the marriage.

When the family learned that Billy had made it home, Stephan slipped down to his friend's house and broke the news of Lucy's marriage as gently as he could. Billy, still reeling from the shock of his mother's death, flung himself out of the house when he heard the news and sailed off in his father's Bugeye. When he returned at dawn the next day, he was very pale, and there were new lines in his face that would never wear away. But his manner was calm, and he greeted the newlyweds with polite if insincere wishes for their health and happiness.

A few years rolled by. Billy and Charlie were polite to each other when their paths crossed, but they never renewed their childhood friendship, although Stephan was a frequent guest in Billy's home. Charlie and Lucy's marriage was not blessed with children, and Billy often wondered if Lucy was happy. Sometimes he caught her looking at him wistfully when they passed on the street. But being an honorable man, he ignored her glances and stayed away from the blacksmith's house.

Then civil war broke out between the states. Billy was a Union supporter from the start. He went north to Pennsylvania as soon as war was declared and joined the Union Army with his father's blessing. Charlie left home a month later, traveling to his mother's family in the South, where he joined the Confederates. Billy saw a lot of action, and his bravery in battle earned him several promotions within the ranks. He was a sergeant in the Federal Army of the Potomac, serving in the Union I Corps under Joe Hooker when Lee entered Maryland.

At dawn on the morning of September 17, 1862, Billy's unit was sent to engage the Confederate troops gathered near Antietam Creek. After marching through the North Woods, they emerged into a cornfield. In front of them, Billy could see the glint of Confederate bayonets through the tall stalks of corn. He was not the only one to spot the menace. General Hooker immediately halted the infantry and brought up four batteries of artillery, shooting shell and canister over the heads of Billy's unit, covering the field.

An artillery duel erupted, with the Confederates returning fire from their horse artillery batteries to the west, and from four batteries on the high ground across the pike from the Dunker Church. The Union troops retaliated, using nine batteries on the ridge behind the North Woods, to support the four 20-pound Parrott rifles that Hooker had employed when he spotted the Confederate ambush.

The artillery and rifle fire from both sides acted like a scythe, cutting down cornstalks and men alike. Every stalk of corn in the field was razed, and the slain lay in rows precisely as they had stood in their ranks. Then Hooker's troops advanced, driving the Confederates before them.

At one point, Billy looked up from the fighting and recognized a tall, broad-shouldered figure in gray standing along the Confederate line. For a moment, among the terrific storm of shell, canister, and musketry, Charlie and Billy stared at one another.

. . . And then, with a suddenness that ever-after haunted Billy's dreams, Charlie's head was blown off by a shell. For a few seconds, the tall figure remained upright, still clutching his Richmond Musket; then Charlie's blood-stained, gray-uniformed body slowly crumbled to the ground. Billy gave a shout of horror, but there was nothing he could do, and so he turned grimly back to the task at hand.

Less than two hours after the attack began, Billy lay in the cornfield semiconscious, with a shattered bone in his right leg, a bullet wound in his left thigh, and another in his side. He didn't remember much after that until he came to in a medical tent several days after the battle. He felt gaunt and weary and old, but there was still air moving through his lungs and he could hear the sound of the wind.

Billy was invalided out of the armed forces and sent home to Annapolis. The doctor had managed to save his shattered leg, but he would walk with a limp the rest of his days. Stephan dropped by the night he came home and commiserated with Billy as one gimpy-leg to another. They spoke briefly—very briefly—about Charlie and the widowed Lucy, who was coping well with her bereavement. Stephan was now earning enough through his carving to support the family so he had moved himself, his mother, and his sister into their own home, not wishing to be a burden to Charlie's relatives.

About a month after Stephan moved his family into their new cottage, Billy received a formal invitation to dinner. He felt a little awkward about accepting it, for it meant seeing Lucy for the first time since Charlie's death, but his father urged him to go.

The awkwardness between Billy and Lucy upon their meeting over supper lasted about a minute before they fell into easy conversation. By the end of supper, Stephan, Billy, and Lucy were laughing and talking in a manner they had not used since before Billy left on his fateful sea voyage so long ago.

Billy never officially started courting Lucy, but he became a frequent guest of Stephan's at the little cottage, and he would carry Lucy's packages home for her whenever they met in town. He wondered a little at the increasing frequency of these "accidental" meetings, but he did not speak of them. Some lingering loyalty to Charlie kept him silent.

One early morning, as Billy made his sleepy way down to the docks through the fog, the mist around him started to swirl in a strange manner. The temperature dropped ten degrees from one step to the next. Billy shivered and rubbed at his arms as he turned the corner. Then he stopped dead, his eyes fixed on the tall, headless, blood-stained figure wearing the uniform of a Confederate soldier that loomed out of the fog in front of him, clutching a Richmond Musket in its torn hands. Billy recognized the figure immediately. It was Charlie. He gave a startled gasp and backed away as the phantom staggered forward one step, two. Then it vanished into the fog.

Billy was shaking from head to toe, unable to run or scream or do anything but stand there staring into the slowly evaporating fog. Only when the sun came bursting from behind the clouds and warmed his skin did he slowly continue his way to the dock.

Two days later, as Billy poured the last of his fresh oysters into the market stall where they were to be sold, he looked through the side window of the stall and saw the same headless, bloodstained soldier stagger toward him through the crowd. No one else seemed to notice the phantom, which walked right through carts and stalls and even people's bodies without regard.

"Some fresh oysters please, Billy," a sweet, much-loved voice called from the front of the stall. Billy tore his gaze from the ghost and looked into Lucy's big brown eyes.

"Certainly, madam," he said gravely, serving her with cautious politeness. He wasn't sure he wanted Charlie's phantom to see him with Lucy.

"You're very solemn today," Lucy said, cocking her head flirtatiously. "Is something wrong?"

Billy glanced uneasily out the window. The headless phantom was gone.

"Nothing's wrong," he told the pretty woman whom he had always loved. "I'm just tired today."

"You need a good meal," Lucy said firmly. "Have supper with us tonight and bring your father."

Billy pictured the determined way Charlie's ghost had staggered toward his oyster stall, but his fear lessened as he looked into Lucy's luminous eyes. He smiled at her and agreed to come. After fixing a time, they parted.

Billy and his father dressed in their Sunday best for supper that evening. Billy's father felt it was something of an occasion, since for once he did not have to put up with Billy's mediocre cooking. They walked down the shadowy lane in the growing dusk, talking shop and trying to guess what would be on the menu.

Stephan's cottage was the last house on a small cul-de-sac. As they approached, the lights went on in the front window, illuminating a headless, blood-stained, gray-uniformed figure carrying a Richmond Musket in its torn hands. It stood on the front porch, waiting for Billy and his father.

Billy's father took one look at the phantom and gave a holler of pure terror. Billy had to grab his father by the arm to keep him from fleeing. He was growing tired of the phantom's appearances and was determined to face it and find out what it wanted.

At the sound of his father's scream, Stephan and Lucy came rushing out to the front porch. Stephan saw the phantom first. He gasped and tried to thrust Lucy back into the safety of the house, but she twisted around in his hands and looked over his shoulder.

"Charlie!" Lucy cried, recognizing the headless figure immediately. She pushed Stephan gently aside and stepped onto the porch. "What are you doing here?" she asked the ghost. She was shaking from head to toe with fear, but her voice was

THE HEADLESS CONFEDERATE

gentle. The headless phantom dropped the rifle and started wringing its hands.

"What's wrong, Charlie?" Lucy asked again. She looked at Billy, who nodded to her, trying to send some of his strength to his brave, beautiful woman. The phantom noticed Lucy's sidelong glance. It turned toward Billy, then reached out and took Lucy by the hand. She shuddered at its touch, but bravely allowed it to lead her down the steps to Billy. Reaching out with his other hand, Charlie's ghost took Billy's free hand and placed it in Lucy's. For a moment, the three of them stood frozen in a tableau, the young man and woman clasping hands within the grip of the headless phantom. Then the ghost vanished, and the phantom rifle lying on the porch disappeared with it.

After a stunned pause, Stephan cleared his throat and said, "Well, that settles that. Sister, why don't you bring your young man and his father in from the cold?"

Lucy, tears streaming down her lovely cheeks, squeezed Billy's hand tightly and then led her betrothed and his father into her house for supper.

4

Dead Man's Coat

CRISFIELD

The whole dad-blame thing started when my wife tore up my favorite coat. She said it was a disgrace and cut it to bits one afternoon while I was out at the market picking up supplies. I got home to find my coat in little pieces, and my wife dusting the parlor with the largest of them.

I had been very fond of that coat and I was pretty mad when I saw what she had done. We had some sharp words about it. The missus got the best of the argument, as usual. Finally, I marched through the back door in a foul temper, grabbed my tackle, and went out on the bay to do some hook-and-line fishing and a lot of sulking.

I've been a waterman since I was a tiny lad, and not a day goes by that I don't get out on the bay, rain or shine. I find it soothing to be out on the water, even when I don't catch a dad-gum thing. My joints are a bit stiff now, and my hands are pretty gnarled up with arthritis, so I don't go crabbing with my boy more than once or twice a week. The other days, I take my tackle and do a bit of fishing after lying a-bed 'til almost eight o'clock. My son likes to tease about that. Calls me a man of leisure.

My wife wasn't surprised to see me heading out in the boat after our argument, even though it was just a few minutes before supper was due on the table. After forty years of marriage, she knows me pretty well and can tell when I need some time alone to work the ire out of my system.

The fish were biting pretty good that evening, and I felt myself relaxing as my bait bucket emptied and my Bugeye filled up with fish. *Maybe the wife was right*, I mused. Maybe it was time for a new jacket. The other one was more holes than cloth, and had so many patches it was difficult to see what the original material had been.

My thoughts were interrupted by a thudding sound on the side of the boat. Startled, I put aside my line and looked over the edge into the horrible, bloated face of a corpse. My stomach heaved as it always did when this happened, but I'd been on too many rescue boats in my time to take fright at the sight of a drowned man. This one was probably leftover from that Baltimore pleasure boat that went over in a sudden squall last month.

I threw a net around the figure, strung the rope through the pulley, and hauled the body in hand over hand. Then I laid him out on the bottom the boat. Poor lad looked young. And he was wearing a rather handsome coat that was just my size. *Well, well*, I thought, *good timing, that. He wouldn't need that coat again, poor boy.*

It would be disrespectful to go back to fishing again, so I pulled in my lines and headed home. After stashing the nice coat in the house, I called the sheriff and asked him to come pick up the body. The sheriff would be able to find out who he was and notify his kin. My duty done, I went home to a late supper and some apologetic cuddling with the missus.

I gave the new coat to my wife the next day. Told her I'd found it floating in the bay and asked her to give it a good washing. It was the truth, in a way. I had found the coat floating in the bay—it just happened to be attached to a dead man. My wife accepted my story without comment. Over the years, I'd found so many strange things floating in the waters that a coat seemed unremarkable.

The coat cleaned up beautiful, and I wore it to town that evening to visit with my grandkids. It was nearly as comfortable as my old one, and far grander. My son called me a toff, and the grandkids each tried on the coat and trailed around the house putting on airs and giggling. I was pleased with my new garment and brushed it off carefully before hanging it up on a hook when we got back home.

It was around three in the morning when I was wakened by a cold breeze rushing over the bed. The missus turned over immediately and went back to sleep, but I lay awake, shivering like a newborn calf in the snow. I pulled the covers tighter around me and rubbed my arms to warm them. And that's when I saw a light bobbing near the ceiling of my bedroom.

I stared at the blue glow, my body trembling with superstitious fear. I had never seen anything like it before. Then the light expanded, getting larger and larger until it became the figure of a young man. He floated a few feet above the bed and looked at me with sad eyes. I choked and swallowed, wanting to run, but where could I go? I couldn't leave the missus alone with this strange phantom.

Then the ghost spoke: "Give me back my coat," he said in a rather posh voice. I was startled by his words. His coat? Then I realized that this must be the ghost of the drowned young man I had pulled from the bay the night before.

"Go away," I said, shutting my eyes firmly and pulling the covers over my head.

"Give me back my coat," the ghost repeated, but I turned over and shoved the pillow against my ears, ignoring it.

After a few moments, the blue light disappeared, and the missus and I were alone again in the bedroom.

I slept fitfully the rest of the night and got up early to look at the coat. It was a real good one. I'd never be able to afford another like it. I muttered an apology to the drowned young man's departed spirit, but I was determined to keep the coat. He'd just have to understand.

I went out on the skipjack with my son that morning and forgot all about the ghost I'd seen in the night—until he appeared in the bow right next to my boy. I gasped, and my son turned to see what was wrong, his elbow passing right through the ghost's chest.

"What's the matter?" he asked me, waving an inquisitive arm through the ghost's head. Apparently I was the only one who could see it.

"Nothing," I said briskly, returning my attention to the jimmies—that is, the male crabs—I was sorting for weight and size. My son shook his head and went back to fixing a crab pot that had gotten tangled up on the bottom of the bay. When I glanced to the front of the boat again, the phantom was gone.

I stewed over the whole thing as I worked the crab pots. It seemed that the ghost had a bee in his bonnet about that coat. I couldn't blame him much; it was such a grand coat.

But still, what use did he have for it now? He should just go on to glory and leave be!

I shook off the incident and finished the day in a cheerful mood. But somehow, I knew that ghost wasn't done with me. I donned the new jacket after I'd washed the crab smell off of my hands and walked home, whistling cheerfully in spite of the strange, cold breeze that swirled suddenly around me as soon as I was out of sight of my son. Ambling down the lane toward my house, I saw a blue light bob out of a tree. It kept pace with me as I walked, slowly growing into the posh form of a young man.

"Give me back my coat," the ghost said as we strolled along the road. The hairs on my arms and neck were prickling with fear. I didn't think the ghost was going to hurt me, but my body hated occupying the same space with something so alien. The chilly wind cut through me like a knife, in spite of my grand coat. I shivered, clung stubbornly to the jacket for another moment, then ripped it off and threw it sideways at the phantom.

"Take the dad-blame coat then, and good riddance!" I shouted. As soon as it hit the ghost, both coat and phantom disappeared, and I was left alone on the road. Slowly, I started walking again, chilly now in the early autumn air, not sure how I would explain the absence of my new coat to the missus.

I waited until after I returned home from hook-and-line fishing the next night and then spun a tale of a large wave that had swept the coat overboard after I'd laid it on the rail to keep it clean. My missus took the news calmly and then said,

DEAD MAN'S COAT

"Actually, I'm a bit relieved. You see, I bought you a new coat the day after I cut up your old one, and I was afraid to give it to you when you came home with that posh jacket you found in the bay."

I gaped at her in astonishment, and then broke out into a happy grin when she pulled a new coat from the closet where she'd hidden it. It was the spittin' image of the jacket she'd torn up for dusters, without the holes and patches, and I loved it at once.

Well, well, I thought, as I tried my new coat on. *The phantom has his posh coat back, and I have a new favorite jacket. Things worked out fine after all.*

5

Open Grave

VENTON

Cancer took hold of my sister real quick the summer I was nineteen. I was still living at home with my folks, but Rachel was married and lived on a farm just outside of Venton. Her husband ran off when she took sick; seems they hadn't been getting along too well, though Rachel had never complained to us about it. Anyway, Rachel had no one else to turn to, so we brought her home and took turns nursing her and amusing Little Lacey, her four-year-old daughter.

It was hard watching my big sister dying by inches. Rachel grew pale and thin, until she couldn't get out of bed. She went from feverish to freezing cold in an instant, and we had to carry her out to the privy because her legs would no longer bear her weight. Little Lacey wanted to play with her mama and didn't understand why she couldn't. It was almost as hard to hear the little girl crying as it was to see Rachel gasping in terrible pain. The doctor kept her drugged up as much as possible to ease her discomfort, but she hated the vagueness it caused, hated not recognizing her own family. She would take the medicine only when the pain became unbearable.

At the end, Rachel faded away. She was a pale ghost, her fair hair scattered across the pillow and her blue eyes focused already on a horizon we could not see, and where we could not follow. We set up a cot in the kitchen so she could be at the center of the family action. She liked to watch Mother cooking, Father reading the newspaper, and me sewing or knitting the clothing I sold to the local shops. Little Lacey would perch beside her mama, brushing her mother's fair hair and singing songs to make her feel better.

One midsummer night, Mother and I sat with Rachel as she drifted off to sleep, listening to her breathing become faint and watching the lines of pain fade from her face as she stepped across that divide that every human must one day cross. We each held one of her hands and cried together when she was gone.

Father dug a shallow grave for her in the family plot at the back of our property, and all our friends and neighbors came to comfort us as we lay Rachel to rest. Little Lacey didn't understand what had happened, and kept asking everyone she saw where her mama had gone. No one knew how to answer her.

It was about a month after Rachel died that I looked up from my sewing to see a thunderstorm blowing up right quick. Little Lacey was playing out back, and Mother and I ran outside and called for her to come in. Mother's got a bad hip, so she sent me to search for the child before she got herself hit by lightning. I raced toward the copse of trees behind our house, calling for Lacey. Then I saw a chubby figure come rushing out of the woods near the family graveyard, her fair hair blowing wildly in the heavy wind whipping ahead of the thunderstorm.

"Aunt Sadie, Aunt Sadie!" I heard her little voice calling to me above the rush of the wind and the almost continuous roll of thunder. I dropped to my knees and caught the little girl in a hug, noticing that Lacey was trembling with excitement.

"Aunt Sadie, I saw Mama back there!" Lacey pointed toward the graveyard and then tugged my hand. "Come on. Hurry. She said she couldn't stay very long."

My body tensed, and icy fingers seemed to trail up my arms and legs when I heard her words.

"Lacey, honey, we have to go inside. It's about to storm," I protested, but the little girl broke away from me and ran back toward the family plot in the woods. I followed and reached the fence around the graveyard just as a flash of lightning lit the sky directly above us. In that flash, I caught a glimpse of Rachel's grave, the ground all dug up and the lid of her coffin open. Standing in front of the tombstone, one foot inside the coffin and one out, was a glowing white figure with its hand outstretched toward Lacey.

"No!" I screamed. "No!"

Speckles of light winked all around my eyes in the aftermath of the brilliant lightning flash as I leapt forward and grabbed Lacey. The child kicked and screamed when I dragged her toward the house, refusing to look back at the graveyard. "Put me down! Put me down," screamed Lacey. "Mama says I'm to go back with her!"

The deluge began before we reached the house, but I was already soaked by the child's tears when she realized I would not let her return to her mama. Little Lacey sobbed out the whole story to Mother, who was horrified by the tale and sent her quickly upstairs to change. I didn't tell Mother what I had

OPEN GRAVE

seen, for fear that speaking the story aloud would somehow make it true. Mother must have guessed something of the truth from the look on my face, but she didn't press me for details. She was frightened, too.

After the storm, Father walked all around the property cleaning up debris. He came back to the house to tell us that the water had washed the dirt away from Rachel's grave, and he'd been forced to dig the hole deeper this time and rebury her. Mother and I carefully did not look at each other while he related this strange occurrence.

I kept a close watch on Lacey over the next several weeks and would not let her play in the woods again, no matter how much she begged. Day after day nothing happened. Gradually I relaxed my vigil, deciding that I must have imagined the whole incident in the graveyard. That dazzling lightning flash had played tricks with my eyes, that was all.

One afternoon in early fall, Father hitched up the wagon and went to town. He asked me to go along, but I had a backlog of sewing to do, so he took Little Lacey instead. As they drove along the lane past the copse of trees where the family graveyard stood, a furry white animal—Father never knew exactly what it was—came running out of the underbrush and spooked the horses. They reared up in the traces and then took off in fright. Little Lacey was thrown from the wagon before Father could catch her and died instantly of a broken neck. It was exactly one month to the day after we'd seen Rachel's spirit beckoning to her from the open grave in the family cemetery.

6

Big Liz

CAMBRIDGE

The Master thought it rather strange that so many of his shipments to the Confederate Army were intercepted by Union soldiers. At first, he put it down to coincidence. But it happened one too many times to be just serendipity or a lucky guess by the Union soldiers. Someone was spying on him, the Master decided, and he was going to find out who it was and deal with them mercilessly.

The Master was a firm supporter of the Confederate president, Jefferson Davis, and had committed to send as much food as he could to the Southern army. He was dead-set against the notion of freeing the slaves, and hated the Union president, Abraham Lincoln, passionately. Some of that hatred was now transferred to this unknown spy who was supporting the North.

The Master came up with a short list of suspects—men and women who knew about the shipments or were entrusted with their delivery. He watched each of them closely and paid a few of his loyal men to do likewise. It did not take him long to find the culprit. It was one of his slaves, a behemoth of a girl named Elizabeth whom everyone referred to as Big Liz. The Master himself actually followed her to a rendezvous with the

Union soldiers and listened as she betrayed him to the North. Lying among the bushes, he grit his teeth and forced himself to remain calm. Now was not the time to confront her; not with two armed men present. He might accost her on the way back to the plantation, but he was not certain that this plan would work to his advantage either. He'd once seen Big Liz pick up two full-grown pigs, one under each arm, and cart them over to the slaughterhouse without assistance. He'd have to kill her with his first shot, or she would take him to pieces.

The Master trailed Big Liz home thoughtfully, a plan forming in his mind as he walked silently from shadow to shadow behind her. He hated this traitor-girl as passionately as he hated Lincoln, and he did not want a quick and painless ending for her. No. Something more . . . treacherous was called for.

The Master summoned his trusted men to him and changed the date and time of the next Confederate food delivery, unbeknownst to Big Liz. Then he approached the giant girl and asked her to assist him with a special task. He told her that President Jefferson Davis had entrusted him with a large chest full of gold. To keep it out of Yankee hands, he wanted to bury the chest where it would never be found.

The girl's eyes gleamed when she heard this false report. The Master knew she was already planning to betray the existence of the chest to the Yankees. His heart burned in anger, but he remained calm, fingering his sword in a manner that should have warned the girl as to his feelings—but she took no notice.

The Master had Big Liz carry the heavy trunk—filled with rocks rather than gold—several miles out into the swampland behind the plantation. She was sweating and swearing to herself by the time they reached the secluded glen where the Master intended to carry out the execution. The Master asked Big Liz to dig a deep hole for the trunk, and he sat at his leisure while she worked and strained for hours against the muddy ground, which kept oozing back into the hole.

"Master, this ain't no good place to bury money," she complained once, rubbing her face with dirty hands and leaving a streak of mud on her nose.

"You keep digging and leave the thinking to me," the Master snapped, fingering his sword. Big Liz caught the gesture this time, and she shivered a little in the muggy heat of late evening. She turned back to her task, shoring up the hole with bits of wood and stone to keep the mud from oozing in. She was completely exhausted when the Master decreed the hole to be large enough for his war chest. Wearily, she dropped the shovel on the edge of the pit and pulled the heavy chest down until it lay at her feet. Then she started to climb out of the deep hole. But the Master barred her way, and Big Liz gazed up at him in sudden fear as he loomed over her, his head just an outline against the gibbous moon, his eyes two blazing sparks of light.

"Traitor! Yankee spy!" The Master hissed the words as he drew his sword. "Did you think I would not find out? Fool. There is only one path open to a traitor, Elizabeth."

Big Liz gasped and cowered back into the hole as the Master swung his sword at her. The sharp edge cut clean through her neck, and her head went rolling away into the tall grass as her body toppled across the chest full of rocks. With a sigh of satisfaction, the Master cleaned his sword on the grass and then used the shovel to heap dirt upon the chest and the slave girl who had betrayed him. Briefly, he considered finding her head and burying it in the pit with her body, but it was too dark to go wandering in the dangerous marshland, and he knew that scavengers would make short work of the head when they found it.

The Master whistled cheerfully to himself as he made his way home in the darkness. There was no one now who could stop his shipments to the Confederate Army. As he moved through the dark swamp, he became aware of a prickling sensation at the back of his neck, as if someone were watching him.

The Master knew this was all nonsense, but nonetheless he began to walk faster as clouds swirled across the moon, obscuring its light. The wind picked up, strangely cold on this warm night. The Master's teeth chattered as a breeze cut through him like a knife . . . or the sharpened blade of a sword.

Suddenly, his straining ears picked up the sound of footsteps on the path behind him. Someone was following him! The Master picked up his pace, jogging now through the hummocks and tall grass of the marsh. He could plainly hear his pursuer, who was keeping pace with him easily. Too easily. No man could possibly move that quickly in the tall weeds and shifting wet ground of the marsh that surrounded the path on both sides. The Master was filled with a terrible, superstitious dread as he began to think of demons and witches and other terrible creatures that could steal the soul from a man.

He broke out into a panicked run, fleeing up the path as fast as his legs would carry him. To his utter relief, he saw the lights of his house rise before him, and he knew he was safe.

Dashing past the stables, he rounded the back corner of his house and slid to a horrified halt before a massive, dirt-encrusted figure that glowed with blue fire. The smell of rotting leaves and marsh grass filled his nostrils as his eyes raced up and up the

BIG LIZ

tall creature until they rested on the stump of its neck, where a head had resided only an hour before. Then he heard a chuckle from the creature's side, and he saw the phantom's head tucked under its arm.

The Master stumbled backward, gabbling desperately in fear as a large hand grabbed the collar of his shirt and pulled him upward. As he swung in front of the terrible figure, the ghost stooped and tenderly placed her head on the ground. Then her massive free hand came up and snapped the Master's neck in two. Dropping him to the ground beneath his bedroom window, Big Liz gathered up her severed head and vanished into the darkness.

There was an outcry the next day when the Master was found dead and Big Liz missing from her post. The authorities considered the vanished girl their prime suspect and disregarded the frenzied story told by a frequently drunken footman who claimed that he had seen Big Liz's headless ghost kill the Master.

The authorities searched for months for the Master's killer, but in vain. There were a few faithful men who knew of the Master's plan to lure the slave girl away from the house with a false chest of gold, but they told no one, for fear that the ghost of Big Liz would come for them too.

They say that on the anniversary of her death, the ghost of Big Liz can be seen roaming the swamplands near her old home. Anyone foolish enough to walk near her grave will be driven away by the phantom, who to this day still believes herself to be defending the place where Confederate gold is buried.

7

The Life Car

OCEAN CITY

When my son returned from a long business trip to the Middle East, he was as anxious to spend some quality time with me as I was to spend it with him. My little boy was a tall man now, with a good head on his shoulders and a good career. I was very proud to be his mother, and not afraid to tell him so.

My boy arranged a series of outings for us, and we gallivanted all around southern Maryland, visiting antique shops, browsing in bookstores, and eating ice cream. One afternoon, he proposed that we spend some time on the boardwalk in Ocean City. I chuckled a bit. It had been years since I'd seen the glitz and glitter of the boardwalk. It might be fun.

We piled into his car and giggled like little kids as we drove the familiar road to Ocean City. I'd taken my boy there as a child so he could play on the beach and swim in the chilly waters of the coast. When Ocean City got too built up and crowded, I switched our excursions to the Assateague Island National Seashore, with its wild ponies and beautiful long beaches. But we still occasionally went to the boardwalk to play games and ride on the roller coaster.

I'm a bit older and creakier these days, so we decided to forgo the roller coaster on this particular excursion. We did play some of the games and stroll along the beach—and of course, we ate big, drippy ice-cream cones. My son was edging me slowly toward the far end of the boardwalk, and I could see he had some further agenda on his mind. *Now, what was he up to?*

I eventually saw the first of the white display cases near the end of the boardwalk, and I knew what this day was really about. My boy wanted to visit the Ocean City Life Saving Station Museum. *I should have known!* He'd been crazy about lighthouses and beach rescues and lifesaving ever since he became a lifeguard back in high school.

Still, I felt a bit uneasy as we meandered in the hot sun through the cheerful, laughing, shouting crowd that populated the walkway. I'd heard something about the museum lately from a friend who collected stories about Ocean City. *Now what was it?*

It came back to me as we paused to examine a giant anchor perched outside the building. *Oh, yes!* My friend had heard that the ghost of a little drowned girl haunted the museum. Apparently, a psychic paying a visit had picked up a strong sense of the girl, and the museum staff speculated that she may have been one of the victims of a shipwreck who had not been rescued on time. According to my friend, when the museum had had the interior staircase painted, the footprint of a little girl had been found on the top step, even though the museum had been locked up right after the painter finished his work for the night. *Spooky*, I thought, shivering.

My son dragged me over to look at a 1,210 pound tiger shark enclosed in a glass case near the museum entrance.

According to the information presented with the exhibit, the shark had been caught in the waters off of Ocean City by Grace Czerniak of Buffalo, New York, who fought the shark for three and a half hours. There were no scales large enough to weight the fish at Ocean City, so the shark was transported to a nearby poultry plant for weighing.

Well, good for Mrs. Czerniak, I thought. *Better her than me!*

Then my son escorted me into the museum, guiding me through a little gift shop to the counter at the back, where a charming lady sold us two entry tickets. I glanced around surreptitiously to see if the spirit of a little girl was lurking anywhere, but apparently she was taking a nap. There wasn't even a cold spot in that bright, charming room.

Feeling more relieved than disappointed, I made my way through the curtain separating the gift shop from the museum and entered a room filled with light and color and interesting artifacts. A "Sands from Around the World" exhibit encouraged us to compare Ocean City's sand with that of other places throughout the world. And an Aquarium Room was filled with interesting creatures indigenous to the Ocean City waters.

I wanted to linger in the Aquarium Room, but my son was anxious for me to move on. Urging me past a narrow staircase—*was it the one with the ghostly footprint?*—he escorted me into a room dominated by a huge surfboat. I stared around in wonder, realizing why my son was so excited about visiting this place. I learned later that this exhibit featured one of the finest Life-Saving Service collections in the country. I wasn't surprised. Pictured around the walls were dramatic scenes of wrecks and rescues. Along with the surfboat were an apparatus cart, Lyle guns, a breeches buoy, and a large metal submarine-like object that I could not readily identify.

I turned right when I entered the room and circled the white surfboat in wonder. My son made a beeline for the interactive exhibit and began pressing buttons. As I examined the stories recorded on the walls behind the surfboat, I heard the voice of a man talking about life cars, which was what they called the bullet-shaped object I'd seen to my left when I entered the exhibit.

I listened absently as the speaker discussed what the life service men would do when a ship wrecked close to shore and the seas were too rough for boats. The men tried to reach stranded mariners by stringing a strong hawser line from the shore to the ship. To propel the hawser to the ship, the rescuers would shoot a messenger line from a cannon-like Lyle gun into the mast of the wrecked ship. From there, the sailors were able to pull out the heavier hawser.

Once the line was secure, a life car could be pulled back and forth between the wreck and the safety of the shore. According to the speaker on the video, the life car could be hauled over, through, or even under the seas. However, there was one hitch. After the hatch in the top of the car was sealed, there was only enough air within the device to accommodate eleven people for three minutes. It was hard for me to envision eleven people crowding into the metal car's small compartment, but apparently people in extreme circumstances were not too particular about the manner in which they were rescued.

Life cars were heavy and difficult to handle, and they were eventually replaced by the breeches buoy. A breeches buoy resembles a life preserver ring with canvas pants attached. It could be hauled out to the ship by pulleys. Endangered sailors would step into the buoy and then be pulled to safety. A beach apparatus cart carried all the equipment needed to rig the breeches buoy and could be pulled by the crew or horses to the wreck site.

After hearing about the various pieces of equipment used to rescue shipwrecked sailors, I was eager to examine them for myself. As I rounded the far side of the surfboat, I was struck by a chill in the air. *Someone must have turned up the air conditioning*, I thought. I was shivering as I stopped to examine a replica of a breeches buoy, which was close to the interactive exhibit my son had been using. On the far side of the kiosk was the metal life car. When I drew near it, the air around me grew damp, as if a thunderstorm were approaching. *Strange*, I thought vaguely. Most of my mind was caught up in wondering if I would have been brave enough, amid pounding seas, roaring waves, and a listing ship, to insert myself into the small life car.

I stepped up to it and directly into the coldest air I'd ever felt in my life. I gasped in shock, the air driven right out of my lungs, and glanced through the opening at the top of the life car into the bullet-shaped interior. I found myself staring into the pale, soaking-wet features of a half-drowned sailor who was curled up inside the life car. His hat was plastered to his hair, his skin was deathly white, and his clothes were dripping with sea water. For one terrible moment, I could hear the drip-drip sound of sea water hitting the metal floor of the life car.

I reeled away, bent double with fear and horror. When I glanced back, the life car was empty and my son was hurrying toward me.

"Mom, Mom! Are you all right?" he demanded, clutching my shoulders. "You're shaking like a leaf!"

"Get me out of here," I said in a breathless whisper. "I want to go home, right now!"

One look at my face convinced him of my seriousness. He hustled me out of the exhibit and through the curtain into the cheerful little gift store in the entryway.

"That was quick," the lady at the desk said, glancing at us curiously.

"No time to linger today, I'm afraid," my son said, keeping his arm firmly around me and pushing me gently past the bookcases and out the door.

In the warmth of the summer sun and the hustle and bustle of the boardwalk, my fear slowly faded away. I had ceased trembling by the time I got to the car, and I was able to tell my son what I had seen as we drove home. He whistled softly as I described the ghostly sailor in the life car. He hadn't seen anything either time he looked inside it, but he believed my story.

"It must have been a resonance or a ghostly echo from one of the shipwreck victims who once rode in that particular life car," he concluded. "I've heard that objects can be haunted."

"Well, this one certainly is," I said emphatically. "I feel sorry for the poor man, whoever he was, but I don't ever want to see him again!"

"I don't blame you," my son said. "I wouldn't either."

We finished the drive in reflective silence, and when we got back to my house, my son came around to open my car door and escort me up the steps. Before we parted, he gave me a kiss

THE LIFE CAR

on the cheek and said: "I promise, our next excursion will not have any ghosts!"

"I'm going to hold you to that," I said. He chuckled at me and whisked out the back door and into the car.

It may be silly of me, but I confess that I've never gone back to the Ocean City Life Saving Station Museum since that day, and I probably never will. One ghostly encounter was enough.

8

Ghost in the Mizzen

BALTIMORE

It was Christmas Eve about eight years ago when the ghost first appeared aboard our vessel. I was boatswain back then. My ship was sailing out of Baltimore, circling the globe looking for trade goods. The night was cold, with a stiff breeze, and the sea was high. We had the royals and topgallant sails stowed and altogether it was a pretty wild ride.

It was after midnight. The watch had just been relieved, and Jim Barnet took over the wheel. None of us liked him much. He was a rum sort—a regular crank. The sailors were plenty nervous when he was around.

We had a lot to cope with, riding those high seas. None of us was expecting it when Jim Barnet gave a mighty yell, grabbed a life buoy, and threw himself over the rail into the boiling waters below. I dropped the rope I was coiling, utterly shocked by what I'd seen. "Man overboard!" I bellowed. Hard on my heels, Taylor, the second mate, gave a shout to man the boats. We had the lashings cut in a jiffy and lowered the boats.

We swept the sea around our ship for nigh on four hours before we found Barnet. He had his arms through the life buoy and was completely senseless. At first we thought he was dead, but the captain kept pouring brandy into him while we rubbed life back into his cold limbs. All at once, Jim reared up on the bed, looking as wild and frantic as he had at the wheel and shouted: "The ghost! The ghost! It's the devil. Take him away!" He kicked and shrieked and cursed and writhed like a madman. It took three of us to hold him down until he collapsed against the bedsheets in exhaustion.

I tell you what, folks, we were scared as anything. What had Jim Barnet seen up top that was so frightening he threw himself overboard? *Was* it a ghost? Or the devil? Were we sailing a doomed ship?

The captain was a religious chap, and he scoffed at our fear. "He didn't see anything up top," he growled. "It was his conscience got him in trouble tonight. God sent him a vision as punishment for getting drunk or gambling or something of that nature."

He dismissed most of the men crowding around, leaving just one of us to guard Barnet's bunk in case he came to and began railing again.

It was about 6:30 pm the next day—Christmas Day—when Barnet next awoke. Me and the mate were sitting next to him at the time. He grabbed me by the hand and cried, "Dick, has he gone?"

I eyed him warily. I was pretty sure he was talking about the ghost. I replied soothingly, "Yes, he's gone, mate. We ain't seen him at all."

"Did ya check the mizzen? I see him now, up the mizzen. The devil! The devil's ghost!" Jim's voice rose with each syllable until he was screaming. All hands in the forecastle had crowded around Barnet's bunk when they heard his voice. I heard the sailors murmuring to one another as Jim fell back with a gasp. Sailors are a superstitious lot, and several men scurried away to have a look at the mizzen.

They were back in a jiffy, and they looked nearly as scared as poor old Jim. The mate was shaking from head to toe as he exclaimed, "Dick, it's true. There's a ghost up there. You go look!"

"There ain't no such thing as ghosts," I said dismissively. But I knew the men wouldn't settle down until I looked, so I went topside, expecting a practical joke. It wasn't a joke. The moon was full and illuminated the mizzen clearly. And right there, grinning down at me, was a white figure with the face of a devil. I stood frozen, gazing up at the eerie sight until the captain strolled by and asked me what I was looking at.

"I'm looking at a ghost," I gasped through a tight throat and gestured upward.

The captain glared at the white figure and then glared at me. "Utter nonsense," he barked. "Can't you tell a practical joke when you see one? You go up one side and I'll go up the other and we'll catch our trickster, lickety split."

"I ain't going up there!" I cried. My knees had turned to water at the sight of the devil ghost. I could barely stand, never mind climb. But Taylor was working nearby. He overheard the captain's order and volunteered to take my place.

So up they went, Taylor on one side and the captain on the other while I watched from below. The longer I watched, the more I became convinced of the ghostliness of the figure. Every time one of them drew level with the grinning devil, it vanished like smoke and appeared a moment later somewhere else in the rigging. They climbed up and down and across, trying to reach it, but never came near enough to make a grab for the phantom.

Finally, the captain came down, swearing worse than I'd ever heard him afore. "Call all hands, Mr. Taylor," he barked. "Let's see what rascal is up in the rigging. If I catch him, he'll regret it."

We mustered all hands on deck. All were accounted for, and yet above us we could still see the devil ghost grinning and pointing at us. The crew was terrified. The men wouldn't go aft to take the wheel that night, so the officers had to steer until the ghostly figure vanished from view.

It was a right pretty mess we had on our hands. The sailors were convinced we were on a doomed ship, and no swearing, lecturing, or direct orders would convince them otherwise.

The next evening the steward caught a glimpse of a white ghostlike figure vanishing out a porthole when he stepped into the pantry. A quick inventory showed the remains of the Christmas ham had vanished. "I don't think ghosts eat ham," the steward said. That got a chuckle from the men before the mast. Somewhat reassured, some of the sailors returned to their duties, although some of them thought it was the steward himself who ate the ham.

The ghost appeared in the mizzen again that night; up and down and all around the rigging, grinning its devil grin. The captain was furious. He tried to shoot the phantom, but every time he raised his six-shooter, the ghost danced about, vanishing from one place and appearing another.

"I've got an idea," Taylor said to me. "If the skipper can keep the ghost's attention on himself and the gun, I'll climb up the main and down the stays and drop a bag over his head. That should catch him."

GHOST IN THE MIZZEN

"If he can be caught," I muttered. I didn't believe in ghosts, but that grinning devil face was making me doubt myself.

Taylor just laughed, and we went to share the idea with our captain. He agreed at once.

For the next ten minutes, the captain and the ghost sparred with one another, guns waving, fingers pointing, swearing and dancing about. Meanwhile, Taylor climbed stealthily upward and then made his way to a spot just above the grinning ghost. He dropped the bag over its head and collared it.

"It's real," he shouted at once for the benefit of the watching crew. Then he swung and slid his way down to the deck as the sailors cheered in the moonlight.

We crowded around and watched Taylor open the bag. A glistening white face blinked peacefully up at us. It was our monkey Jenny. She was covered head to toe with white paint and held a gnawed hambone in her hand. The men exclaimed and laughed. I felt like a fool. I'd come *that close* to believing in ghosts, and it was just Jenny all along.

It took a moment for us to realize that we'd been laying food and water out for her like clockwork, but no one had actually seen the little creature for several days. We reckoned Jenny must have fallen into our paint tub just before Christmas and had stayed aloft since then because she was too embarrassed to be seen.

The captain was so annoyed I thought he'd toss our pet overboard, so I gathered up the creature and took her below to the little nest she'd made for herself. I briefly considered showing her to Jim but figured he wouldn't understand what he was seeing—and worse, it might scare him further. Barnet babbled and thrashed and screamed every time he woke up.

In the long days that followed, it became evident that Jim Barnet had gone completely insane from his scare and the long hours spent in the cold sea. We were forced to leave him in an asylum when we docked at Cape Town. It was only at the end of our journey that we learned that Jim Barnet was an escaped convict sentenced for manslaughter. He'd mistaken the monkey for the ghost of his victim, and it drove him insane.

9

The Well

SOUTH MOUNTAIN STATE PARK, BOONSBORO

What I remember most about that fatal day at Fox's Gap were the sounds and the smells. I could smell the acrid artillery smoke, the hot and heavy stench of blood, the damp odor of freshly turned earth and ravished vegetables—all that was left of the farmer's fields. And the sounds . . . oh, the sounds! Rapid gunfire, agonized screaming, cursing, yelling, bullets whistling above and around me. I was fighting to hold off the attacking Union soldiers, side by side with the other North Carolina Confederates serving under General Sam Garland. My best friend Mark and I, along with several buddies from our brigade, were trying to hold the old stone wall on Daniel Wise's property that September morning. All in vain.

I don't really remember what happened to me at the end. Mark was blown to bits by a shot from a cannon. I think I was shot in the back of the head. One moment I was fighting hand to hand with a handsome blue-eyed Yankee boy who was cursing at me with an Ohio accent, and the next I was floating above the battlefield, looking down upon the devastated remains of Daniel Wise's farm. The torn-up fields were strewn with the bodies of dead and dying soldiers, and Fox's Gap had become a no-man's land with soldiers from both sides taking pot shots at one another.

At twilight, Union General Reno arrived on the field to assess the situation. He was impatient to march on Turner's Gap, and he rode north to reconnoiter, right into General John Bell Hood's Texas Brigade. By the time darkness ended the day's fighting at Fox's Gap, Reno was mortally wounded and the Texans withdrew to Boonsboro, leaving the Union IX Corps in possession of the field.

Frankly, I wasn't sure why I was still there. My body was stacked atop Mark's corpse behind the Wise house, awaiting burial when the fighting ceased, and I figured it was time to move on. I'd always thought I'd head straight up to heaven when I died, like they taught us in Sunday school. None of my teachers had ever mentioned that a person's spirit hung around to watch the end of a battle. But apparently you can't will yourself upward, though I tried several times during the night.

The next day saw the victorious Union soldiers swarming over the field, digging rough holes and dumping bodies into them at random. The way they treated our dead was disgusting. I realize that they were exhausted and demoralized by their grisly duty, but it was still very disrespectful.

Then, to my everlasting horror, the Yankees gathered up the last fifty-eight bodies—including the ripped-apart remains of Mark's body and my own—and dumped them willy-nilly into the well just prior to leaving the property. I was outraged and followed after the soldiers, ranting furiously and taking a few swings at them with my fists. Other than shuddering from the cold when I'd plant one on them, the soldiers ignored me entirely.

A sort of heaviness fell on me then, and I sat down next to a large tree to rest. Time passed; I don't know how much. Finally, I stood up, noting that it was almost sundown, and started walking up the Old Sharpsburg Road toward the ruined Wise Farm and my poor discarded, disrespected body. It wasn't long before the bullet-riddled cabin came into sight, and the stench of rotting flesh—most of it buried just a foot or two below the surface of the ground—filled the evening air.

I saw the figure of a man sitting on the porch of the cabin, smoking a pipe. To my surprise, I recognized the man as Daniel Wise, the owner of the devastated farm where we had fought and died over the possession of Fox's Gap. I'd seen Old Man Wise on the morning we'd commandeered his farm, watching in horror as we ripped apart his land to set up firing lines, position our artillery, and dig in behind the stone walls bordering his property. The last I'd seen of him, he was loading up a wagon with some precious possessions and his children and hurrying away as fast as he could drive.

Apparently, more time had passed as I sat under the tree then I had realized, if farmer Wise was home. Then I received a second shock. Daniel Wise slowly removed his pipe from his mouth, his eyes widening as he stared at me. This was the first sign I'd had that a living mortal could see me. I walked closer, stepping into his yard as the farmer paled with fright.

"Wh . . . who are you?" he managed to gasp, rising from his rocking chair. I wasn't prepared for the question. I didn't want to give him my first name—which was also Daniel—I was afraid it might confuse the issue. And for that matter, what was the issue? Would talking to this farmer free my spirit for heaven?

The silence lengthened uncomfortably. The farmer was obviously terrified by my presence. His face was white, his body was trembling like a sapling in a high wind, and he nearly dropped his pipe twice.

Suddenly, I knew what I should say to this man. I drew in the ghostly equivalent of a deep breath and spoke, my voice sounding cold and hollow: "Our lives were taken from us, and we were not given a proper burial. Be sure that I will return here every night until we receive the honor due us as fallen soldiers."

At my words, the poor man shivered as if he'd been struck by a winter breeze. Looking away from him, I glanced over at the well where my body and those of my comrades had been dumped so roughly. When I turned back to the farmer, he was rubbing his eyes in a puzzled manner, and I realized he could no longer see me. After a moment, he hurried over to the well and wrestled off the wood cover. A horrendous smell of putrefaction billowed upward, causing the farmer to fall to his knees, coughing and gagging.

Before my startled eyes, I saw writhing black shapes, barely recognizable as the spirits of my fallen companions, bursting out of the top of the well, wailing and moaning and shrieking in remembered agony and fear and outrage. The misery and hopelessness of the sound drove me to my knees. It was obvious that Farmer Wise heard it too, for he clapped his hands over his ears, falling facedown into the overgrown grass at the base of the well. After several terrifying moments, Wise staggered upright and clapped the cover onto the well. He fled then into the house, and I heard him push something in front of the door.

Things went heavy again for me, and my surroundings blurred. When next I came to my senses, I was back under the tree by the side of the road, feeling a strong compulsion to walk up to the Wise Farm and speak with Daniel about the proper burial of the Confederate bodies in his well.

Over and over again I made this trek; I lost count of how many times. Sometimes I saw the farmer walking about outside. Sometimes I sensed him waiting tensely inside the farmhouse for me to leave him in peace. Sometimes I saw him leaning on a hoe in his kitchen garden, staring at the old well with a look of misery on his face. I wondered if he, too, could hear the muffled howls and moans I heard reverberating beneath the cover.

Old Man Wise acted uneasy in my presence, but never as frightened as he had the first time we met. I never saw him go near the well, and I did not approach it myself. The agony in that area of the farm was acute, and I was reluctant to disturb it.

I don't think Daniel Wise was indifferent to our plight. A few times, I slid through the walls of the cabin after darkness fell, and I saw him writing letters to the officials in Washington, D.C., demanding a proper burial for us.

I don't know how much time passed, but one day I awoke beneath the tree at noon rather than sunset, aware that something momentous was taking place. I hurried down the road and found the Wise farm awash with uniformed men digging up graves and tenderly placing the remains they found into specially prepared boxes. I ran to the well and saw men carefully lifting one decayed corpse after another to the top. I recognized one of them as my own—don't ask me how, for it was rotted beyond all reckoning. Daniel Wise watched the bustling scene from the porch, a look of grim satisfaction on his face.

THE WELL

I walked slowly up until I was standing in front of him and said: "Thank you."

I am not sure if he saw or heard me, but something must have reached him, for he relaxed a bit, took out his pipe, and nodded a few times toward the spot where I met him each night.

"Rest in peace, young soldier," he said. "Rest in peace."

At that moment, I heard someone call out, "Daniel."

I thought at first it was one of the farmer's family members speaking to him. But the farmer didn't stir, and I realized he hadn't heard anything.

"Daniel," the voice called again. It was a man's voice, and tantalizingly familiar. And then: "Come on Danny-boy. Are you going to linger here all day?"

I recognized the voice then and whirled around. My best friend Mark hovered a few feet above the ground in front of the cabin, grinning from ear to ear. His body was glowing, and an unearthly radiance filled the air around him.

"Let's go home!" he said, beckoning to me with a happy grin.

"Home," I repeated longingly, staring at the radiant brilliance behind him. Now this was more like it. Heaven, here I come! I followed my best friend into the light and did not look back.

10

The Ghost House

DORCHESTER COUNTY

Well, now, my friend Roy the blacksmith lived in a ghost house, don't ya know. Lived there his whole life along with his Ma, his Pa having gone to Glory when Roy was just a little tyke. Not a night passed when the spoons didn't rattle in the drawers all by themselves and the blinds crash down on the windows as soon as you walked into the front hall and whip back up when you walked out. Pictures whirled back to front and front to back while you watched them. And every night at seven o'clock, you could hear the sound of footsteps coming down the staircase and into the parlor. The rocking chair by the fireplace would creak as if somebody had just sat themselves down in it, and then the room would start to smell of pipe tobacco, even though nobody in the family smoked.

It was enough to drive an ordinary man mad, but Roy and his Ma liked it. They considered the ghosts good company and would chatter away to them while they sat at the kitchen table or played checkers around the fireplace at night. They love to show off their ghosts to folks visiting from out of town. People'd come for miles around to "ooh" and "aah" when the pictures flipped and the blinds shook and the spoons rattled in the drawers.

Well, one day Roy up and told his Ma that he'd decided to marry his sweetheart, a rosy-cheeked tanner's girl named Bessie who lived in the next town over. Roy's Ma approved of Bessie in general terms, but she'd heard from the cousin of her neighbor's friend that Bessie was a-feared of ghosts.

"You'll never get that one to set foot in this house the way it is right now," his Ma said to Roy. "You'll have to choose between Bessie and the ghosts, or buy yourself a new house."

"I ain't buying a new house," Roy said firmly. "And I don't plan to kick out the ghosts neither. You let me think on this a piece, and I'll come up with something."

Roy thought and thought for a good week about the problem while he worked in the forge, shoeing horses, and making iron rims for the local wheelwright.

"I got me an idea," he told his Ma one morning. His Ma was right glad to hear that. Roy'd been so caught up with his thinking, he'd been mighty poor company all that week. She pestered him to tell her his idea, but Roy refused 'cause he didn't want her to laugh at him if it didn't work.

The next morning, Roy went out to the small hill in back of his house with a mess of timber he'd bought the day before from the mill. On that hilltop, Roy built a small two-room cottage with an overhead loft. In the front room, Roy put some snappy old blinds in the windows and large pictures on the walls and a creaky old rocking chair in front of the little fireplace. In the kitchen he put a big chest of drawers and filled them up with spoons. Then Roy built a broad staircase leading up to the loft, with bouncy steps that squeaked whenever he set foot on them.

Upstairs he put a small bed with a nightstand topped by a pipe holder and a pipe cleaner.

When the new house was finished, Roy went down to his place and stood in the center of the parlor.

"Ghosts!" he shouted. "You've been mighty good friends to me. Now I aim to be a mighty good friend to you. Most men would have conjured you out of their house when they brought a new missus home, but not your friend Roy. No, I made you a brand-new house for your very own, and I put it right at the top of the hill so you have the best view in the county! If you meet me here at midnight, I'll take you up to your new house."

Roy's Ma came out of the kitchen and shook her head. "It'll never work," she told Roy. "We're going to have to ask the conjure-man to get rid of the ghosts."

"It'll work," Roy assured his Ma.

At eleven fifty-five that night, Roy came down from his bedroom on the second floor and stood by the front door, waiting for the ghosts. The last five minutes ticked by slowly, and Roy was afraid that maybe his plan wouldn't work after all. Then, precisely at midnight, all the blinds in the front hall whipped up with a bang, and the spoons started rattling in the drawers. The pictures flipped back and forth so fast that they made a little whirlwind that knocked over his Ma's flower arrangement, and footsteps came down the staircase and paused right in front of Roy.

"Thank ya, ghosts," Roy said humbly. "My future missus and I thank ya kindly for this."

Then Roy opened the front door and led the way up the hill behind his house. Behind him, he could hear the soft thud and swish of ghostly feet moving through the grass. He opened the cottage door, hung his lantern on a hook, and built up a fire. Around him, he could hear the tentative rattle of the spoons in the kitchen drawers, and a blind snapped up with a loud bang that was even noisier than the sounds made by the blinds in his house. Footsteps went up the staircase to the loft, and he heard a distinct chuckle from overhead when the pipe-smoking ghost found the new pipe holder and pipe cleaner on the nightstand.

A moment later, footsteps came down the squeaky staircase, and the rocking chair by the cozy fireplace creaked and began to rock back and forth. The smell of tobacco smoke filled the air, and a ghost began to hum happily beside the warm fire. On the wall opposite the rocking chair, a picture flipped to the back side and then flipped to the front.

Roy swallowed a lump in his throat and stepped to the middle of the room.

"Ghosts," he said, pulling his Bible out of his pocket, "I swear on the good book that this is your house to do with as you please. I'll keep it fixed up for you and will come visit you as often as I can. We will live side by side for the rest of my days."

All the blinds shot up at once, the spoons rattled loudly, the pictures whirled around and around, and a voice from the empty rocking chair said: "Amen!"

Roy went down to his now-silent house and told his Ma that the ghosts had moved to their new home. She didn't believe him at first, until a whole day had passed without a single spoon rattling or picture whirling, and without any tobacco smoke wafting from the rocking chair by the fire. "Well, I guess you done it," his Ma conceded. "But it's mighty lonesome here now without our ghosts."

THE GHOST HOUSE

Roy married Bessie and brought her to his home. Roy's Ma and Bessie got on like a house afire, but Ma still missed the ghosts. Several times a week, she would take her knitting and climb the hill to the ghost house to sit by the fire and pass the time of day with her old friends. And when Roy's little ones got big, they would visit the ghost house with her and laugh and laugh at the spirits' antics.

Bessie never would set foot in the ghost house on the hill from the day she was married 'til the day she died, and Roy left the ghosts up on the hill out of loyalty to her memory, even after she had passed. It wasn't until Roy went to Glory himself that the ghosts returned to the old house in the valley to live with Roy's oldest boy, and they've been there ever since.

11

Ghost in the Chimney

FROSTBURG

I once heard tell of a family living just outside town that lost everything when their house was struck by lightning during a thunderstorm and burnt to the ground. They couldn't afford to build another house and had to settle into a run-down cottage where an old bachelor had just passed away. There were only a couple of rooms in the place, but somehow the Clintons managed to squeeze themselves and their six children into the cottage, and there they stayed.

Now, roly-poly Mr. Clinton was working as a tinsmith. He didn't make much money at his trade, being more of a dreamer than a craftsman. For years, he'd wanted to buy a little shop and set up a bakery like his father had done before him. He'd come home every night after work and try to make the perfect sweetbread. His goal was to create a secret formula that would make the Clinton fortune. Unfortunately, all of his experiments tasted like sawdust (which was the reason his father had not taken him into the family business in the first place), but he kept on trying.

Now, Miz Clinton was as thin and spare of frame as her husband was round and jolly. She was a very good cook indeed and would have been a welcome addition to her father-in-law's bakery if she hadn't been too busy raising six children to work outside the home. As it was, she spent every spare minute in her own kitchen, cooking over the woodstove or mixing and kneading dough for bread. So it was Miz Clinton who first saw the ghost in the chimney.

The stove had been placed in front of the old fireplace, and its pipe ran right up the flue. Miz Clinton was looking straight at the fireplace when the ghost stuck his head right through the brickwork and glanced around the kitchen.

Miz Clinton dropped her spoon into the pot of chowder she was stirring and clutched at her heart as the ghost walked out of the fireplace and leaned reflectively against the wood piled next to it. It was the ghost of an older gentleman, as lean and spare as Miz Clinton, with a wild thatch of white hair and a wrinkled, nut-brown face. He adjusted the wire-rimmed spectacles perched on his nose so he could look more closely at the fireplace flue, taking no notice of Miz Clinton.

"Now where in tarnation?" the old ghost asked. He bent down and peered intently at the flue and then said, "Oh, I see. It's still in there. Dad-gum! I can't go to my rest until it's found."

The ghost thumped his hand against the brickwork, and it went right through all the way up to his shoulder. "Nobody's found you and I can't rest," he wailed, following his arm into the fireplace until he disappeared completely.

Miz Clinton was "took strange" by the appearance of the ghost, and she staggered over to her rocking chair and sat fanning herself while she recovered from the encounter. What in the world had the ghost been talking about? It sounded as if he'd lost something. But what could it be?

The older children weren't expected home from school for another hour or two, so Miz Clinton wrapped up the baby and went over to the neighbor's house to tell her what had happened.

"Sounds like Old Man Mueller," her neighbor said when Miz Clinton described the ghost. "He was a strange fellow, no mistake. Folks thought he was a bit of a miser. Maybe he left some money behind when he died! If he shows up again, say 'In the name of God, what do you want?' That's the way to get a ghost to talk to you."

Miz Clinton nodded solemnly, and repeated the words over and over to herself on the way home. That night, after the children were asleep, she told her husband about the ghost. Mr. Clinton laughed, a deep rich chuckle that reverberated along the floorboards. "A ghost, eh?" he said disbelievingly. "Well, my pretty, if you find his fortune, I won't have to finish concocting my special recipe, and where's the fun in that?"

"If I find a fortune, we could buy ourselves a nice bakery and you could work on your recipe all day long," his wife retorted.

Mr. Clinton laughed delightedly over the idea and waltzed his wife around and around their bedroom until they were both overcome with mirth. But the idea wouldn't leave Miz Clinton, and she was determined to speak to the ghost in the chimney if he ever appeared again.

About a month passed without incident. Then, one night, Mr. Clinton was mixing up a bowl of his latest sweetbread concoction when the ghost stuck his head right through the bricks of the chimney.

"The Lord bless my soul!" exclaimed Mr. Clinton. A religious man, this was the closest he ever came to swearing. When she heard her husband's words, Miz Clinton came running in with the baby.

The ghost had extracted himself from the chimney and was now examining the flue carefully through his wire-rimmed spectacles.

"In the name of God, what do you want?" Miz Clinton called breathlessly, jiggling the wailing child on her hip.

The ghost of the old man blinked a few times and turned to look at her, as if he had just noticed that she was in the room.

"Madam, I am looking for my money," the old man's ghost said with dignity. "I placed all my savings in this chimney. If you remove the third row of bricks from the bottom of this flue, you will find it right where I left it the day before I died."

"The third row of bricks," Miz Clinton repeated.

"Yes. Right down there," the ghost said, pointing toward the bottom of the flue. He took no notice of Mr. Clinton, who stood paralyzed with fear, his wooden spoon dripping batter all over the kitchen floor.

"I would be obliged if you would remove the money right away," the ghost added. "My spirit is tied to this place until the money is found."

"Yes, of course," Miz Clinton said. "Right away. Thank you!"

The old man nodded to her and then walked through the brickwork of the chimney and vanished.

"Wh . . . wh . . . That . . . that . . . " stammered Mr. Clinton.

"Yes, dear, that was the ghost," said Miz Clinton calmly, taking the dripping spoon from him and handing him the

GHOST IN THE CHIMNEY

wailing baby. He took the little girl from her automatically, still staring bug-eyed at the fireplace, and began jiggling the baby absentmindedly to stop her crying.

By the time the baby was quiet, Miz Clinton had pried almost all the bricks from the third row from the bottom of the chimney flue. Hidden inside the flue were four gallon jars packed to the brim with money.

"The Lord bless my soul!" Mr. Clinton exclaimed, three times in a row out of sheer surprise.

"Yes, dear, I believe he has," said Miz Clinton calmly, carefully counting out the money on the kitchen table.

There was enough cash in those gallon jars for the Clintons to buy both a new house and a new bakery, with so much to spare that they were able to send their older children to a fancy boarding school to be educated. Mr. Clinton divided his time between working the cash register and trying to make the perfect sweetbread recipe, while Miz Clinton baked wonderful cakes and cookies and pies and breads for them to sell. The children all volunteered to be taste-testers for their mother, but none of them were brave enough to try their father's concoctions. Roly-poly Mr. Clinton never did concoct the perfect sweetbread, but in spite of this minor setback, the family managed to live happily all the rest of their days.

12

The Music Lesson

BALTIMORE

She had not been studying organ long, but already she loved it passionately and her teacher said she had talent. With enough application, the girl could easily win a scholarship to a prestigious music school. She had a small practice organ to use at home, but the girl needed more experience playing a large pipe organ, so her teacher arranged for her to practice each evening at the church near her home. It was a lovely church, and the girl knew it was an honor to be allowed to play their world-class organ. But something about the lonely, nighttime practice sessions frightened her. She hated walking through the empty sanctuary after dark. It felt as if invisible eyes watched her from the shadows. She never felt safe until she was actually in the organ loft.

One twilit evening in late spring, the girl hurried into the churchyard, cradling her organ books against her chest. She had an audition the next week and needed to spend every spare minute practicing. As soon as she stepped onto the porch, her skin prickled and goose bumps rose on her arms. Her hands trembled as she turned the key in the lock. The thought of walking into the dark sanctuary made her knees buckle. *Don't be ridiculous*, she told herself, raising her chin and straightening her shoulders. Still, it took an effort of will to push open the heavy door. *Courage*, she thought, and stepped inside.

The girl marched bravely through the foyer and into the echoing sanctuary. Its huge stained glass windows loomed dark and bleak in the twilight. Long vacant pews swept out in every direction, a stark reminder that she was alone in a building built to hold hundreds. There was an air of watchfulness about the huge space; as if an invisible presence observed her every move. Her footsteps rang through the sanctuary as she walked up the center aisle. Small hairs rose on the back of her neck, and she hugged her organ books closer. The church was so very large and so very empty. Anything might be hidden in the dark shadows that lurked in each corner. She quickened her pace.

The girl began to relax when she reached the staircase leading up to the organ and gave a sigh of relief when she stepped into the loft. She put her books down on the organ and arranged herself on the bench, shivering a little in the sudden cold that swept around her. It was strange to feel such a chilly breeze on a warm night in June, she thought, feeling spooked.

The girl was about to put her feet on the pedals when suddenly a single pure note came from the organ. She froze in place and stared wide-eyed at the keyboard, which had just played all by itself. The chill around her increased perceptibly. Shudders of cold and fear shook her from head to toe. In that moment, she was convinced that she was not alone in the echoing darkness of the empty church.

A sudden movement by the stairs caught her eye, and the girl turned her head. Standing behind her was a portly, middle-aged woman in a long, light blue dress. The woman was flickering in and out of existence like a bad filmstrip, and she was translucent. The girl could see the steps right through the phantom's body. The woman seemed to be staring at something . . . or someone. . . sitting on the bench with the girl.

Chills rippled through the girl's chest as she remembered the strange note that had come unaided from the organ. The air shimmered around her as if she was caught in a heat haze, but the temperature was so cold that the air clouded with vapor when she exhaled. The pedals suddenly moved under her feet and a chord sounded spontaneously from the organ. The girl gasped in fear as the organ keys pressed themselves without her assistance.

Convinced that she was occupying the same space as a ghostly organ student about to have a music lesson, the girl leapt to her feet and fled for the staircase, even though that meant heading straight toward the other phantom. Head down, eyes on the floor, the girl ran right through the flickering woman. For a moment she was enveloped in a terrible cold that made her limbs shake and her stomach do flip-flops. She screamed in terror and kept running. She raced down the staircase, down the echoing center aisle of the church, and out the side door. It slammed behind her, loudly enough to wake the dead in the churchyard. She flinched but didn't stop running until she reached the safety of her own bedroom. There she lay panting on her bed, her body trembling with fear, and vowed to never step foot in that haunted sanctuary again.

In the morning, she told the whole story to her organ teacher and drew her a picture of the flickering phantom woman. The ghost was quickly identified as a deceased church organist who sometimes gave music lessons at the church.

THE MUSIC LESSON

In spite of protests by her music teacher and parents, the girl was so unnerved by her experience that she quit playing the organ and pursued a business degree when she went to university the next year.

13

Traitor

CLINTON

She could remember being happy. Somewhere, back behind the pain, she could remember laughter and pride and good hard work. She stood on the stairs staring blankly into the room below, trying to recall how she had come to this place. What had happened to her?

The house seemed familiar. She gazed around thoughtfully as her misty form slowly solidified. Oh, yes, of course! She recognized this place. She had once known it very well indeed. She and John had lived here with their three children and had made their home into a tavern, a polling place, and a post office for the local residents. There had been laughter here, and political debate, and later there was support for the Confederate cause against the Yankee traitors who wanted to ruin their way of life. She could recall those days quite clearly, and the memory of them made her smile as she came slowly down the staircase, her ghostly feet barely touching the boards, and began wandering through the rooms.

The house looked different now from the way she recalled it. She frowned, and then a pain drove through her as she remembered why. Of course it looked different. John had died, leaving her alone with three children and too many debts. The house had been rented to that fellow . . . what was his name? Trying to recall her former renter's name was like hitting a blank wall. Behind the wall was betrayal of the worst sort, and an excruciating agony that made her mind shy away from the memory.

"Hail Mary, full of grace," she whispered, crossing herself.

She entered the tavern kitchen, her thoughts turning to a different house—a Washington, D.C., boardinghouse on H Street—that she had run as a widow. She remembered a young actor named John Wilkes Booth who had visited them often and teased her gently as she went about her many tasks. Booth was a Confederate sympathizer, something of which she approved. Her youngest son, John Junior, was a spy for the Confederates and was passionate in his beliefs. Her son found a strong sympathizer in Booth, and the two Johns would discuss politics late into the night.

After a while, her Washington boardinghouse became a general meeting place for several rising young Confederates beside John Wilkes Booth—Lewis Paine, George Atzerodt, and David Herold. She liked having the young people around the place and supplied them with food and drink and a sympathetic ear when it was needed. There was some talk about kidnapping President Lincoln, something she put down to youthful high spirits, until things took a turn for the serious in April.

She ran a semitransparent finger along a countertop agitatedly as she thought about that April. Her very last April, it turned out, although she had not known it would be at the time.

Sometime in early April, Booth and his friends had traveled to her old tavern-home and left a package there that included two carbines and some ammunition. A few days later, they gave her a message to take to the man renting the tavern—what was his name?—since she was running errands nearby.

It wasn't until the news of Lincoln's assassination whirled through Washington that she began putting all the pieces together. Even then, she had not really expected the visit from the investigators. They came twice, and the second time she was taken away with them; charged with conspiracy and with aiding the assassins and assisting in their escape. The picture of John Wilkes Booth that had been placed by her daughter on the mantelpiece and the arrival of young Lewis Paine with a pickax during the arrest didn't help her cause.

She was taken to the Carroll Annex of the Old Capitol Prison and later transported by Colonel Baker in a buggy to the Washington Arsenal Penitentiary, where the assassination conspiracy trial was held. The trial proceedings began on May 9, 1865, and continued until the end of June.

She maintained her innocence over and over again, supported by Lewis Paine. Then the man who rented her tavern—what was his name? John Lloyd—came to the stand. As the memory unreeled before her eyes, she stepped backward as if slapped.

"No! Go away. Leave me alone," she whimpered.

He'd said . . . Lloyd had said that *she* had requested that he have the carbines ready for Booth and Herold when they arrived at the tavern late on the night of the assassination. He claimed that she had delivered Booth's field glasses to him for safekeeping earlier on the same day! But had she? *Had she?* She couldn't remember now. Couldn't remember anything save the way her stomach dropped when she heard the jury pronounce a guilty verdict. Could only remember the way she felt when

TRAITOR

she got her first glimpse of the gallows with the ground so very far below, and how she felt when the noose was placed over her head and began to tighten around her neck.

She gasped desperately in pain and reached out her hands as if to grasp the happiness she had once felt in this kitchen; but she couldn't reach it now, and would never reach it again.

"Dear God. Sweet Mary. Don't let me fall," the ghost of Mary Surratt whispered into the silence.

No one answered.

14

Steal Away Home

BERLIN

I knew Thursday was the day to run—yes, sweet Lawd—when I heard my auntie singing in the harvest field: "Swing low, sweet chariot, coming for to carry me home." That was Moses's song, and I knew it meant that she'd received word that Moses—Harriet Tubman—had made another trip south. If I hurried, I could maybe jump on the Glory Train with Moses and ride "home" to Canada!

My mammy and my pappy had both run north when I was little, and my mammy's sister had looked after me 'til I grew big and strong. My aunt's man had a bad leg and would never be able to run, and she refused to leave him. But she always kept track of the railroad signals, and she'd been teaching me everything she'd ever heard about the way north.

My auntie had a rich, wonderful voice, and she always sang when she worked in the fields. She used the songs to teach me how to escape. "Follow the Drinking Gourd" was the song she used to show me the group of stars that told a-body where the North Star was. "Wade in the Water" taught me to stay near water and jump into it if I heard bloodhounds baying. And whenever she had something new to tell me, she'd sing "Steal

Away Home," and that meant I was to meet her in the woods to talk about the Glory Train.

Sure enough, as soon as my auntie was done singing about the chariot, she started singing "Steal Away Home." Yes, Lawd, today was the day! I met my auntie in the woods after sunset. She'd put together a little bag with my best Sunday clothes to wear when I got to town so I wouldn't look like a runaway slave, and some food. She wrapped me up good in my uncle's jacket, 'cause the winter nights were cold, and she told me to look for a house with a lantern on a hitching post or a Jacob's Ladder quilt hung on the railing; both signs that the place was a "depot" where I could sleep safe for the night and maybe get a good meal.

I kissed my auntie and promised to buy her and my uncle's freedom when I was a rich man living in Canada. Then I ran as softly and as swiftly as I knew how. Moses was meeting a group about two days' north of here, and I had to get there by Saturday, which was always the day that Moses took her passengers north—or risk missing the Glory Train.

I knew the first few miles well, but soon I was in new territory, making my way through swampy land and avoiding the road. My auntie told me it was best to sleep and eat off the land until I reached my conductor. It was cold—yes, Lawd—the coldest winter I could remember, but I kept myself wrapped up good and ate only a little bread at a time. I even found some roots to chew on. It was enough to keep me alive, but it weren't tasty and it didn't keep the rumble out of my belly.

To keep my mind off my hunger, I thought about Moses. Harriet Tubman had been born a slave, just like me, right here in Maryland. She worked as a house servant when she was little and then went out into the fields as soon as she grew big and strong. When she was a teenager, she was hurt in the head trying to protect another slave from an angry overseer, who threw a two-pound weight that hit Harriet instead of the other slave. All the rest of her life, Moses suffered from that head injury, sometimes falling into a heavy sleep right out of the blue.

She later ran away from her master because she was afraid she was going to be sold, following the North Star each night until she reached Philadelphia. Since Pennsylvania was a free state, she settled there and got a job. After about a year, she decided to join the Underground Railroad and help other slaves find their way north. She rescued her sister and her sister's children, her brother, and many others.

I paused to eat a little more of the bread around dusk the next day, and that's when I heard the bloodhounds baying. I hadn't planned on pursuit, at least not right away, but apparently my master had already spread the news that I was missing. I tossed my bread back into my sack and I ran—oh yes, Lawd—I ran as fast as my legs would go, until I found me a stream. I waded until I thought my feet would freeze off, and then climbed from tree to tree like a squirrel before dropping back into the stream to wade some more. I didn't hear them dogs again, but I was so chilled that I knew I needed shelter or I'd die of the cold.

I took a risk and went out onto the road for a while, hoping to find a depot. I couldn't believe my eyes when the first house I saw through the growing darkness had a lantern on the hitching post. I turned into the lane, shivering something fierce, and realized that the house was dark. No one was home. What was I going to do? Them dogs were still out there, and I had to find shelter or at least build me a fire.

As I stood there, too cold and numb to think, I saw a pretty golden-haired lady wearing a long white dress come around the corner of the house. She held a lantern in her hand that lit up her figure until it glowed. I thought she must be an angel. She beckoned to me, and I followed her at once, not doubting for a minute that she would help me. She led me through the yard to an old woodpile. Leaning over it, she pointed to some logs piled in the corner and motioned for me to move them.

The lady held the lantern for me to see while I shifted the logs and found a trapdoor underneath them. I pulled the heavy door open and looked down into a dark pit. The woman lowered the lantern into the darkness, and I saw a ladder and some blankets and in the corner, a canteen of water. I scampered down the ladder right quick, calling my thanks, and heard the trapdoor close above me. Several thumps told me that the lady was piling logs back on top of the door to keep it hidden. In the darkness, I pulled a stub of candle from my sack—the Lawd bless and keep my auntie—and lit it with a match. I drank the canteen dry and curled up among the blankets.

I woke up once, some time later, hearing the sound of baying bloodhounds, but they didn't come near the secret root cellar under the woodpile, and I went back to sleep. The next time I woke, it was because the trapdoor was being pulled open. A young farmer's face appeared in the square of light above me. When he saw me, his eyes widened in shock. He stared at me as if I were a ghost. Finally, after a few ragged breaths, the farmer said: "Son, how did you get in here?"

I was puzzled. Hadn't the pretty lady told her husband I was here? I explained at once about running away, and about the bloodhounds and the pretty lady in white who hid me. Another look of shock flickered over the man's face when I mentioned the woman.

"What's the matter?" I asked apprehensively. The man shook his head and told me it was safe to come in the house.

He hid me in an upstairs room and brought me some hot food. Then he sat in a chair beside me and showed me a small painting of a pretty golden-haired lady wearing a long, white dress. It was the woman who had hidden me.

"My wife," the young man said, tears springing to his eyes. "She died six months ago."

I thought I would die myself, right on the spot, as his words sank into my head. I had been hidden by a ghost! Great Lawd in heaven! A ghost!

"She was the only other person alive who knew about that root cellar," the young man said at last. "I saw her in a dream last night, and she told me that she'd put something in there for me. That was the reason I opened the trapdoor this morning, because of seeing her face in my dream. I hadn't been down there for a good six months before then."

I must have looked as shook up as he was, 'cause the farmer gave me a sip of brandy to steady my nerves and told me to get some sleep. He told me he would hide me under the false seat in his wagon and take me to another safe house after dark. Which was just what he did.

STEAL AWAY HOME

I never did meet up with Moses, but I *did* make it first to Philadelphia, then up to Rochester, and finally to freedom in Canada. Yes, Lawd! It was hard traveling all by myself. It took me a long time—eighty-nine days—and I got plenty tired of swamps and riverbanks and having nothing to eat but roots and leaves. But at last I was free! I found my parents living in Ontario, and we saved up enough to buy freedom for my auntie and uncle and bring them to Canada too. Hallelujah!

15

Handprint

CALVERT COUNTY

We knew something was wrong almost as soon as the first words of the will were read. Justin and I—my name is Alec—exchanged glances, and then looked at our elder brother Harve, who was plainly nervous. His double chin wobbled when he spoke—always a sign of nerves with Harve—and he kept smoothing back his greasy black hair and fiddling with his cuff links. The tone of the will was wrong, and the cadence of the sentences. This document surely had never been written by our father; at least, not the most important bits.

But the lawyer read on, regardless of the growing tension in the room. At the end of the hour, Harve had inherited everything—or at least everything that mattered—of our father's very large estate. Justin and I were provided for, of course; the small plots of land on which we each resided with our families were deeded to us, with just enough money to survive on if we were careful. We would either need to move away and begin again, or depend on our big brother's generosity to maintain our current carefree lifestyle.

This was not at all what our father had discussed with us many times as we were growing up. According to our late father, the property was to be divided equally among us after his death, as was all his money. And I do not think that he changed his mind in the months before his fatal accident; not our unalterable, stern father.

Harve was gloating and condescending in his manner when it became obvious that the lawyers accepted the will as true and final. He assured us in a manner that affronted both of the attorneys that he would help support us just as our father would have wished. Very politely, Justin and I declined his aid. We shook the hands of the lawyers and left the manor house quickly. We did not speak of the matter then. It was only later, after we were calm and both our wives could be present that we discussed the will at length.

All of us agreed that Harve must have gotten a hold of the will and altered it before the lawyer came. Still, it would need a handwriting expert and a lot of money to prove this, and in the current situation neither Justin nor I had the finances to hire a lawyer to contest the will. Besides, our father would turn over in his grave if we were to reveal such a scandal about our family. We finally agreed to pool our money and buy a local mill that was for sale. If we worked hard, we would be able to sustain ourselves and our children without Harve's assistance.

Harve and his wife were scandalized when they found out that we had purchased the mill. Our family had been gentlemen plantation owners for generations and had never soiled our hands with hard labor. Justin and I told them bluntly that father's will had changed all that. Obviously, our father's concern had not extended past the eldest child, and so his two younger sons had to make a different path for themselves.

We irritated our elder brother still further by freeing the slaves that came to us as part of our inheritance—more to drive Harve wild than from a sense of their equality. We employed the now-free men and women in our mill and households in exchange for several small plots of land on which they could maintain a cottage and garden. We also promised each of the former slaves a share in the wages of the mill once it was profitable enough to support all of us. Our abolitionist actions enraged Harve, but there was really nothing he could do about them.

Of course, the people living on the neighboring plantations were shocked by the terms of our father's will and were happily scandalized by our new career. They hurried to move what business they could to our mill so that they could see how two rich young men would cope with a sudden reduction in circumstances. This didn't bother either of us. Let them gawk and give us their money. We'd give them such good service that they would never purchase from anyone else. And this proved to be the case.

Slowly, the nine-day wonder surrounding our father's will died down, and life went back to normal for everyone else. Justin and I learned a new normal—one involving hard work—and we came to appreciate the men whom we had once treated as slaves. Their quiet assistance smoothed over many a small error that we made when we first began working in the mill, and their cheerfulness kept up our spirits. Our wives felt the same way about women who worked with them to care for our small properties and our children. It was during this first difficult year that I became a firm supporter of the abolitionist movement, and even quietly helped several of Harve's slaves make their escape to Canada. It was the least I could do for my kind elder brother.

We didn't see much of Harve after the first several months, when he would come to our homes or to the mill to berate us. We did retain the acquaintance of our wealthy neighbors, who kept us on their calling lists partly to spite Harve. However, our reduced circumstances exposed us to a much wider acquaintance with our middle-class neighbors. To the surprise of both our families, we found that we liked the card parties, village dances, and church socials far better than the formal dinners and balls we had once known. It was a further surprise to us men when our wives went on to take an active roll in both church and town functions. My house was filled up nearly every day with members of the Ladies Aid Society, the Sewing Circle, or the Town Improvement Committee.

All in all, we settled happily into a new way of life, and so it came as a shock when an invitation to go bird-hunting arrived from Harve nearly a year after our father's death. In his note, he expressed a desire to end the coldness that lay between the brothers, and there was something in his tone that conveyed a keenly felt loneliness—and possibly some guilt.

After much discussion, Justin and I decided that our father would probably have wanted us to go. We arrived at Harve's manor house an hour before dawn, walking slowly up the drive through a soft, misty rain and discussing all the small things that had changed about the place. Harve was not as good a manager as our father had been, and there were already signs that the property was in trouble. Old Esau met us at the door and gave us a toothless grin. We smiled back at him with a new appreciation for this faithful old retainer. If I'd had the money,

I would have freed him on the spot and asked him to live in my house and take care of my family. From the look on Justin's face, something similar must have been going through his mind.

We were fitted out with the best guns, remembered vaguely from a life that seemed much further away than a year, and stomped out over familiar pathways in the damp, clinging mist, looking for grouse, partridge, quail . . . whatever birds happened to be on hand. We walked for many miles that rainy day without a single shot being fired. Harve, who had grown enormously fat over the past year, was quickly out of breath and even more quickly weary of our company, for we were not at all interested in his social conquests and affected indifference when he discussed the problems of the plantation. Our lives and beliefs were so different now that finding common ground was nearly impossible. Plus the off-again, on-again drizzle was enough to kill the most cheerful of spirits, and Harve certainly did not possess one of those, being inclined toward the melancholy.

It was Justin who first noticed that we were nearing the field where father had had his fatal accident. Father had slipped suddenly when climbing the fence in front of us and had slammed his head against a large rock on the far side, dying almost instantly. Justin stopped abruptly, staring at the spot where our lives had changed—I was not sure now if I considered the change for the worst or for the better—and perforce we stopped with him. It was at that moment that Harve gave a terrible gasp of fear. I turned immediately to look where he was pointing, and saw a gray figure solidifying out of the fog and drizzle. It might have been a trick of the mist, but I thought I saw the glowing figure of our father standing near the fence where he had died. I heard Justin draw in a sharp breath, and knew then that he had seen the figure, too.

Harve was trembling from head to toe, his rolls of fat jiggling in a most unpleasant manner.

"Father," he gasped, clutching his heart with his free hand.

The glowing figure of our father gestured toward him sternly and spoke in a deep, sepulchral voice that brought chills to my arms and legs.

"Do not continue to wrong your brothers in this way," he commanded in the cold voice I remembered so well. "If you hope for mercy when you die, then you will right this wrong before the clock strikes midnight."

The glowing figure turned and placed his hand on the top rail of the fence at exactly the point where he had slipped and fallen to his death. There came a sudden flash of fire, and the air was choked with a wave of sulphurous smoke as the ghost of our father leapt nimbly over the fence and vanished into the mist. The three of us coughed and gasped in that wretched smoke for several moments. As it cleared, my stinging eyes fell on the fence, and I grabbed Justin on the arm and gestured to it with my rifle. Burned into the upper rail was the imprint of a hand.

Harve took one look at the handprint and bolted back toward the manor house so quickly that we couldn't keep up with him, despite his tremendous girth. He was galloping down the manor drive on his massive horse—the only one on the plantation that could hold his three-hundred-pound body—when we arrived at the house. Justin and I stared after him and then went on into the house to drop off our guns before heading back to our respective homes.

HANDPRINT

The next day, word came to us that Harve had gone to the county courthouse and signed papers that divided the plantation and our father's money equally between his three sons. The money was welcome, of course, and Justin and I were able to bring the plantation back to prosperity between the two of us. But we refused to abandon our mill—signing it over to the men and women who had so ably assisted us when we were down on our luck—and we insisted that all the slaves on our plantation be given their freedom and offered a chance to stay and earn wages or go where they willed as free people. Most of them stayed.

Harve nearly died of apoplexy when he realized he now had to pay for the labor that he'd once had for free, but he'd made such a mess of things on the plantation that he dared not disagree with us for fear we would walk away and leave him to his own devices. Whenever he spoke out against our ways of management, it merely required a short walk out to a certain fence—where a ghostly handprint was permanently burnt into the top rail—to get him to agree to anything we desired.

16

The Ghost of William Jinks

ALLEGANY COUNTY

I did my duty as a sharpshooter for the Union Army during the Civil War and somehow made it through alive. It took thirteen months after I mustered out to be comfortable sleeping in a bed, much to the distress of my dear mother. At first I rolled myself up in a blanket and slept in the yard, but gradually I worked my way onto the porch, then the bedroom floor, and finally to my old featherbed.

That first night in the featherbed was a real treat. I thought maybe I'd died after all and this was heaven. But the second night was different. I woke up shivering in the sudden cold, wondering why the summer night felt so chilly. I rolled over and found myself looking at a glowing figure glaring at me from the foot of the bed. I was never so scared in my whole life. My body broke out all over in goose bumps, and my hair positively stood on end. Still, I'd seen so many horrors during the war, what was one more? Gathering my courage, I exclaimed: "Who are you?"

"I'm Jinks. William Jinks," the specter said in a husky tone with an odd echo to it that made my flesh creep. "I'm the ghost of the rebel soldier you picked off in the battle of Bull Run."

My mind raced back to that fateful day. I'd picked off more than one rebel during that horror. Which one was this? Then I had it. "Are you the chap that hid behind the old log? The one that kept ducking down whenever I took aim? I didn't think I hit you."

"You sure did, seeing as I've been a ghost ever since that day," the specter growled. "I'm here to demand reparation."

"Reparation?" I said indignantly, sitting up and hugging my knees to my chest. "What do you mean reparation? We faced off in a battle. It was a fair fight. I can't bring you back to life."

"You can't," William Jinks said in sepulchral tones. "But there's my widow to consider. I looked in on her yesterday and she's having a hard time getting along. You must hunt her up and tell her to dig the little farm for coal."

My ears perked up. Coal? There was good money to be had in coal. "How do you know there's coal there?" I asked skeptically.

The glowing figure gave an eerie smile. "It is my province to know things denied to you mortals. Now, will you go?"

I considered thoughtfully. I didn't much like my current job, and a potentially rich widow sounded mighty tempting. I loved my mother, but once a fellow has been living on his own, he really prefers his own place. "Where is your widow living now?" I asked.

"It's not far," said the ghost of William Jinks. He gave very specific directions to a place in Maryland. I listened intently and started calculating the cost of taking such a trip. A pretty high sum.

"When can you start?" growled the specter.

I glanced toward the window. The darkness was fading. Sunrise was close. I bet the ghost would disappear with the dawn. "I'll tell you tomorrow," I said just as the specter of Jinks vanished.

I hustled about the next day, making plans. At dinner, I told my mother I'd taken work as a traveling salesman selling patent washing machines. She wasn't pleased to have me gallivanting about the nation, but she knew me well enough not to argue.

I went to bed early that night and waited a long time for Jinks to appear. The first sign of the specter's presence was a plummet in temperature. Then a glowing ball of light appeared at the foot of the bed and burst outward, becoming the figure of a scruffy man in a Confederate uniform. His red-eyed glare was less formidable this evening.

"What have you decided to do?" Jinks asked without preamble.

"I'm heading south tomorrow. I should see your widow in about ten days," I replied. "Do you have a message you wish to send?"

Jinks sat himself down on the bed—or tried too. He sank too deeply into the mattress. "No message," he said emphatically. "As a ghost, I can only appear to the person who caused my death. If I send a message to Lisbeth through you, she'll know you killed me and boy howdy will you get it. She's got quite a temper on her. I've had a hard time of it from Lisbeth now and again. She was always fussing at me. Still, I thought lots of her, and she just worshipped me." He gave a gusty sigh that made the hairs on my neck prickle.

How interesting. William Jinks and his wife didn't get along when he was still in the land of the living. "Why didn't you agree?" I asked curiously.

"Lisbeth was very industrious," Jinks said. "She was always working. And I was born tired. She never understood that. Come to think of it, you may have done me a good turn at Bull Run. Now I don't have to hustle for anything to eat, the heat don't bother me, and I can rest whenever I like. When Lisbeth is provided for, I promise I'll stop haunting you. Just keep it a dead secret that you killed me. Lisbeth loved me to desperation despite everything, and she'd kill you if she knew you done me in and send your ghost a-wandering like mine."

"I'll make sure your widow is provided for," I said vaguely. "And I accept your promise to stop haunting me when I do."

Jinks nodded happily several times and then spiraled away until the room was dark once more.

I left promptly at noon on Saturday and made my way slowly south. I got pretty good at selling the patent washing machine during my journey. If the householders permitted it, I brought the machine inside and washed out a few pieces of their linen to show them how the machine worked. We shared tips on the best methods of stain removal and how to get a collar good and stiff. I became quite the expert in the art of washing.

All of this was good practice for my encounter with Mrs. Jinks. My plan was to ask Mrs. Jinks to board at her place while I sold my washer to the folks in the surrounding county, and I'd ingratiate myself by helping her with the laundry on washday. I figured I had to feel my way carefully before mentioning a possible coalfield. Otherwise, she'd label me a scallywag and send me packing.

Exactly ten days later, I reached the Jinks place in Allegany County, Maryland. I knocked on the door, and it was opened by an old woman. My heart plummeted. I'd been expecting a young lady. The ghost of William Jinks hadn't looked old. But apparently, I'd assumed wrong. Still, I'd given my word to the specter that I'd help his widow, so I stuck with the plan.

"Is this Mrs. Jinks?" I asked politely.

"Lawd, no," the old lady smiled. "I'm Mrs. Freesner that lives with her, now that her husband has passed. Step inside and rest a bit while we wait for Mrs. Jinks. She's running some errands and should be along shortly."

The front room was neat and clean, but there wasn't much furniture. The pieces were rather threadbare and worn, just as I expected from what the ghost of Willam Jinks told me. Mrs. Freesner and I hit it off splendidly. She quickly confided in me that Mrs. Jinks was far better off without her husband, whom she described as the laziest, most shiftless man who every lived.

Mrs. Freesner broke off suddenly and gestured toward the window. "Here comes Mrs. Jinks," she said with a fond smile. I gazed through the glass at a lovely dark-haired woman with bright eyes and a resolute chin. She looked like she wouldn't take any nonsense from a lazy husband, and I liked her the better for it. In fact, I was pretty taken with the widow right from the start. She listened intently to Mrs. Freesner's introduction, and her attention sharpened further when I said, "I had the honor of being connected with your husband William in the late war. It was his earnest desire that if he was killed I should carry a message of his undying affection for you. It has been impossible for me to reach you until now, but please rest assured I came as quickly as I could."

"Thank you very much for your kindness, Mr. Wilkins," Mrs. Jinks said in a low, melodious voice. It gave me a happy shiver to hear her speak. "I am glad to meet someone who knew William during the war."

I winced inwardly at her kind words and felt like a fraud. Still, this was what the ghost of Jinks wanted me to do. Oddly, Mrs. Jinks did not ask for further particulars about her husband, and I didn't pursue the matter. Instead, I described the business that brought me to this part of the country and asked if she would be willing to board me while I worked in the area. Mrs. Jinks was willing to take me on, and though she didn't say so, I received the impression she and Mrs. Freesner were glad for the extra income.

On my first night at the Jinks cottage, I had a spectral visitor. William Jinks appeared at the foot of my bed in his Confederate uniform. I rubbed my eyes sleepily and growled, "What now? I'm here like you asked me to be. Can't you let me sleep in peace?"

"I just wanted to know how you are coming on," the ghost grumbled.

"Well enough so far," I said, sitting up with a sigh. "But it's going to be a slow business breaking the news of the coalfield to her."

"Why is that?" asked William Jinks suspiciously.

"Because she's got to have faith in me, or she'll think I'm telling tall tales," I replied. "If she doesn't believe me, she won't go looking for the coal, and your haunting will be in vain."

The specter was much struck by these words. "That's true. My Lisbeth is no pushover. Still, you should hurry it up as fast as you can. Lisbeth hates to have a man bothering about the place." With that piece of advice, the ghost vanished.

Well, she certainly didn't care to have you hanging about, I thought as I rolled over and went back to sleep.

The next few weeks were the happiest I'd ever lived. I had wonderful luck selling my patent washing machines. When I wasn't traveling around meeting friendly people and making their lives a little bit better, I was doing odd jobs around the house and yard to earn my keep. My mother taught me to make myself useful, and that's just what I did. I repaired the fence, fixed the leaking roof, built a shed, chopped firewood, fixed Mrs. Freesner's spinning wheel, and so forth.

In the evenings, I'd sit with the ladies on the little front porch and tell them lighthearted stories from my days as a soldier. We laughed heartily at some of the antics the men got up to between battles. Mrs. Jinks and Mrs. Freesner countered with stories about the people and animals living in the region, and their tales were equally interesting to me. They helped me feel a part of the community.

The disclosure of the coalfield had completely slipped my mind until a month to the day after my arrival, when the ghost of William Jinks appeared once again in my room.

"What is the meaning of this delay?" the specter demanded. He was so angry that blue sparks shot out of his glowing body in all directions.

"Relax, Jinks," I said uneasily. The ghost was quite disconcerting. For the first time, I wondered if Jinks could actually harm me if I didn't obey his request. "I am going to tell her tomorrow."

"See that you do," the ghost said with a red-eyed glare, "or I'll appear to you while you are with Lisbeth and scare you out of your senses! She'll think you're mad and run you off the place."

"Hogwash," I said.

I decided the ghost was more bluster than business. Still, I'd given my word. It was time to act. And once my part of the bargain was fulfilled, the ghost couldn't haunt me anymore. Jinks had given me his promise.

The next evening, I found Mrs. Jinks alone on the porch. "Mrs. Freesner has gone to the village for a while," she explained.

As always, her melodious voice sent a happy shiver down my spine. I dropped onto the steps at her feet. "I'm glad I caught you alone," I said, feeling awkward. "I've been wishing to tell you something. I've made a discovery while working around your place, and it's something I can tell only to you."

Mrs. Jinks clasped her hands tightly together and I felt her gaze on me. Her eyes were dark and luminous in the moonlight. I felt a bit light-headed with all her attention focused on me. I tore my eyes away and began poking at the ground with a little stick.

"It's just this," I said, addressing the stick in my hand instead of the lovely woman beside me. "I think there is coal on this land, right underneath your house. If this is true, you stand to become a wealthy woman. If you don't have the means to make the investigation yourself, I am happy to advance you whatever capital you need as a partial share in the mine, should coal be found." I reddened and added: "You wouldn't have to pay me back if it's a false alarm. It's just what anyone speculating on coal would do in my place."

Mrs. Jinks straightened herself, and it seemed as if she was disappointed somehow. I turned to look at her. "How do you

THE GHOST OF WILLIAM JINKS

know there is coal here?" she asked. Her voice was cool, and I'd never heard that tone from her before. My heart sank.

"Your husband told me his suspicions about it. I wanted to make sure his idea was correct before telling you. I didn't want to raise false hopes," I explained.

"You are very kind," Mrs. Jinks said, still in that cool tone. "I'll go in now and think it over."

She rose and it felt like a wall had been erected between us. I was devastated. I reached out suddenly and caught her hand. She paused and looked down at me.

"I've discovered something else," I said in a husky voice. "But I am afraid to tell you."

Mrs. Jinks slowly sank down into her chair. Her eyes were suddenly warm, and my heart started to pound against my ribs. She didn't speak, but I could tell she wanted me to continue.

"I've discovered that you are the one woman in the world for me," I said. "But how can I ask you to marry me when you will be rich and I am just a poor soldier who sells washing machines?"

Lisbeth's eyes told me what she thought of that nonsense.

"Will you have me?" I asked humbly.

Lisbeth smiled, and I knelt on the top step and took her in my arms.

"We don't have to do anything about the coalfield," I told her after our first kiss. "We can go north to meet my family and then settle anywhere you like. I can earn a good living selling washing machines."

"Pshaw," said my lady. "Why would we ignore the coalfield? It will be money for our children and grandchildren."

"And Mrs. Freesner will live with us. She'll like having children underfoot," I continued. "I suggest we have a new house built in the town while I take you to meet my family. After that, if you wish, we can begin work on the coalfield."

Lisbeth gave me another kiss to confirm our plan.

"I confess, I feel much better now that you know about the coal," I said. "I feel like Mr. Jinks can rest in peace now that you are taken care of."

"Mr. Jinks," Lisbeth said crisply, "Was always very good at resting. You, on the other hand, are very good at working. Which is why I will have you or none."

This declaration earned her a third kiss.

I waited several hours after I retired for the ghost to arrive. William Jinks swirled into being in a flash of blue light at the foot of my bed and eyed me expectantly. "Did you tell her?" he demanded eagerly.

"I told her," I confirmed. "She is very happy."

The ghost of William Jinks rubbed his hands with glee. "That's good, that's good," he cried. "I'm obliged to you for your trouble, though frankly I don't see how you could have done much less. Still, a promise is a promise. I'll stop haunting you now. You are free to go back north."

"And what are you going to do?" I asked, curious about how a ghost occupied itself once its earthly mission was complete.

"Me? I'll keep Lisbeth company from now on," said William Jinks. "She won't be able to see me, of course, but I'm sure it will gladden her lonely heart to feel my presence in this house. Now, how soon can you leave? I don't wish to be inhospitable, but this house is mine, and I've made arrangements to live here permanently. The sooner you get away, the better."

I was nettled by his obvious desire to be rid of me. After all, I'd done him a favor. "I am going as soon as I can get married," I told him. "In about two days' time."

"Married?" said the ghost. "Well, well. So you found yourself a bride during your stay here! I only hope that you get as devoted a wife as my Lisbeth."

"I am quite sure I have," I said briskly. "And my bride and I will be happy to leave you in possession of these premises."

William Jinks eyed me suspiciously. "Who'd you say you were going to marry?" he asked.

"Lisbeth Jinks," I said.

The ghost of William Jinks reared up in shock and started sparking blue flames from every part of his body. He was furious, and I could tell he wanted to kill me right there and then. But he'd promised to stop haunting me if I did as he bade me, and I knew he couldn't touch me. The flaming ghost of William Jinks lunged toward me, arms outstretched to grab and strangle. I held my ground, sure I was right. Just before Jinks reached me, he hit a wall of pure white energy that flung him backward with such force that he vanished through the far wall.

"Good riddance," I said with satisfaction.

That was the last time I saw the ghost of William Jinks.

PART TWO

Powers of Darkness and Light

17

Goatman

BOWIE

The stories were all over school, though Jill hadn't paid much attention to them. Some crazy creature was stalking people all over Prince George's County. Her friends claimed a mad scientist had been secretly experimenting on goats when he knocked over a critical beaker. The controversial chemical cocktail spewed all over the scientist, sizzling through his skin and entering his bloodstream. The panicked man tried to run away and fell against one of the goat cages. When he touched the creature, the experimental formula combined his DNA with that of the goat. His body mutated, twisting and swelling until he transformed into a monstrous creature—half-human and half-goat. The mutant creature walked upright like a man, but it had a massive human torso, circular horns, and hairy goat legs ending in cloven hooves. Mind snapping under the stress, the scientist roamed the countryside with an ax. He became known as "the Goatman" and there were rumors flying everywhere about his predations and attacks. Jill's friends mentioned decapitated dogs, dismembered humans, murdered hikers. Everyone in the region was talking about the Goatman and the teenagers at her high school were warned to keep watch and report anything suspicious.

All this scary talk didn't interest Jill in the slightest. What did a crazy Goatman have to do with her? She had more pressing matters on her mind, like what she should wear on her date with Nick. This was her first date with the local football star, and she wanted to "wow" him. After several hours and multiple changes, Jill chose a smashing off-the-shoulder affair in the very latest style and spent an hour curling her long dark hair. Then she was ready to go, and just in time too. She heard Nick pull up outside and went to meet him.

"Don't stay out past curfew," her father warned from his spot on the sofa.

"Of course not, Daddy," Jill lied. She was a spoiled beauty who did exactly what she wanted. Her father never checked up on her.

They turned the radio up and sang along to their favorite songs as they cruised to Nick's favorite pizza place. The restaurant was a madhouse that Saturday night. Lots of Jill's classmates were present, sitting in big groups around a cluster of tables or sweet-hearting two by two in the booths along the wall. More than one teenage girl eyed Jane with envy as she cuddled in the back booth with Nick, eating pizza and laughing merrily at his jokes.

After dinner, Jill and Nick went to the movies and did a bit of necking in the back row. When the film was over, Nick eyeballed Jill and slyly suggested that they take the scenic route home to do some stargazing. Jill grinned back at him, not averse to parking with her new fellow.

Jill felt the first hint of unease when Nick turned the car onto Fletchertown Road. This was one of the places kids at school claimed to have seen the Goatman. They said he lived in a cave under an old metal bridge not far from here. But she forgot her worries when Nick found a convenient place to pull off and parked the car under the trees. There weren't many stars to be seen through the thick foliage, Jill noted, but it was dark and private, which made it a good spot for romancing.

Nick gave Jill a brilliant smile and she melted into his arms. The blue outfit was definitely a hit, she decided hazily a few moments later. Jill made a mental note to buy a few more off-the-shoulder dresses as she cuddled close to her boyfriend in the darkened car. They'd tuned into a local station and spent some time necking to the sound of romantic music on the radio.

All at once, a series of loud thuds in the nearby woods broke the silence. The car reverberated with the noise.

"What was that?" Jill cried, jerking her head back in surprise.

A few yards away, the trees and underbrush rustled as if something large was stalking toward the car. Jill heard the terrified screech of a frightened animal. She stiffened in Nick's arms, vividly conscious of their remote location on this stretch of the road. Suddenly, the dark night didn't seem so romantic to her. This was a perfect spot for a deranged madman to lurk, Jill thought, pushing her amorous boyfriend away.

"Someone's coming," Jill said nervously. "We need to get out of here. That Goatman might be around."

"Awe, c'mon babe, it's nothing," Nick said, trying to get in another kiss. She pushed him away again.

"No, really. We're all alone out here. I'm scared," she said, her voice rising in fear.

GOATMAN

"I'll protect you," Nick said confidently, taking her back into his arms. But Jill was no longer in the mood for romance. She was scared and made no bones about it.

"Take me home," Jill cried. "I want to go home!" Her last word ended in a shriek as the car shook as if something . . . or someone . . . had slammed into it. Jill screamed: "Get us out of here now!"

"Jeeze," Nick said in disgust, "just like a girl! It's the wind. The weatherman said there might be thunderstorms tonight."

But he turned the key in the ignition and went roaring out of the lover's lane with a screeching of his tires.

The couple drove home in stony silence, Nick occasionally muttering to himself about the crazy notions of girls. Jill ignored him, just happy that they'd gotten away from that secluded spot.

As soon as they pulled into her driveway, Jill leapt from the vehicle, glad to get away from her disgruntled football star. She slammed the door as hard as she could. And then she screamed.

Nick leapt out of the car, his ire forgotten, and raced around the engine. Catching Jill in his arms, he cried: "What is it? What's wrong?" Then he saw it.

A bloodstained ax was embedded in the back of his SUV, wrenched from the grasp of the insane Goatman who had been stalking them on Fletchertown Road.

18

The White Horse

CAMBRIDGE

He was the rector of a major parish in Cambridge, which had kept him busy from dawn to dusk for nigh on thirty years. And now he had a mission charge in the nearby village, which kept him constantly on the road between the two towns, visiting his parishioners, preaching, and attending meetings. His wife complained that she never saw him; and he acknowledged the validity of her statement but was unsure what to do about it. His flock needed him—especially at this time. They had just lost the Judge, a beloved and prominent member of their community, and many family members and friends needed counseling as they dealt with the loss. The Judge's wife, Emily, was prostrate with grief; so much so that she could hardly rise from her bed. The good rector dropped by daily for nearly a week until Emily rallied somewhat, bolstered by the arrival of her married daughter and grandson.

Two weeks after the funeral, a frantic note arrived at the rectory, summoning the rector to the Judge's household. The rector and his wife drove over immediately and found the house in turmoil. The Judge's beloved white horse had dropped dead in the field, and Emily was in a frenzy.

"It's an omen," she wailed, wringing her thin white hands and rocking back and forth in a chair by the fire. "The horse cannot live without your Papa, and neither can I. I will be the next to die. You'll see."

"Now Mama, don't talk nonsense," the daughter scolded. But the daughter's pale face and troubled eyes told the rector that she too was afraid of the omen. The daughter sprang up in relief as the young grandson showed the rector and his missus into the parlor, rushing away to bring them some tea and biscuits.

The rector's wife put her arms around her old friend as her husband sat down beside them. They talked for a long time, until a bit of color returned to Emily's cheeks and she almost smiled.

"I am sorry I was in such a state when you arrived," the Judge's wife said as they rose to depart. "The white horse's death came as such a shock. It quite overset me."

"Understandable. It was another grief on top of the one already suffered," the reverend's wife said.

"Please realize that the horse's death is totally unconnected to you," said the rector. "You'll be with us for another thirty years; just you wait and see."

"Days," the Judge's wife corrected him. "Thirty days." Her panic had faded, and she seemed resigned to her fate.

The rector just shook his head and repeated his words. He didn't believe in omens.

A flurry of issues arose the next day that required the rector to spend a week in the nearby village, tending to his mission. When he returned home, he found his wife weeding in the garden. Her face was troubled as she greeted him with a kiss.

"What's the problem, wife of mine?" he asked as he settled his belongings into the house.

"I've been over to the Judge's place twice this week," she replied. "Emily is growing pale and thin. She spends hours looking over the pasture to the place where they buried the white horse. I think you should stop and see her when you have a moment."

The rector drove to the Judge's house the next afternoon. The Judge's married daughter met him at the door. There were dark rings under her eyes, and her whole body trembled. She beckoned him into the kitchen and shut the door.

"Mama keeps talking about the white horse. She says she can see him trotting down the road each evening, pulling a black carriage. My son has also seen the white horse grazing in the field near the barn, just like it did in life. It troubles me, Reverend," she said, setting a teacup in front of the rector. "Do you think it is a death omen?" She carefully poured tea into his cup as she spoke, but her hand shook so much on the last phrase that tea sloshed out onto the table. She exclaimed in frustration and mopped up the spill.

The rector didn't know what to think. He didn't believe in ghosts or bad omens. But it would not do to say so aloud to this poor troubled daughter. He brushed at the tea stains on his jacket as he pondered what to say. "Perhaps it is a good omen," he replied at last. "Maybe your father has sent the horse to watch over you."

"Like a guardian angel?" the daughter asked, perking up at the thought as she poured more tea into his cup.

"Exactly," said the troubled rector, wishing that he could believe it himself.

After he finished his tea, he went to visit with Emily. She sat in a front parlor in ruffled pink skirts and dainty shoes. She was much paler and thinner than she'd been a week ago. She was knitting as she gazed out over the front pasture where the white horse was buried. After their greeting, Emily resumed her seat and said, "I am not afraid to go, rector. The Judge will come for me himself and we will be together again. Do not fret on my behalf. I've lived a good life."

This was not the most promising way to begin a conversation, the rector thought wryly. Instead of trying to dissuade her of the notion, he turned the talk to the many happy stories from a long lifetime of marriage with her venerable and rather oddball husband. Emily was smiling when the rector left the house. As he untied his horse from the hitching post, he looked over the twilight pasture. A flash of white flickered in the corner of his eye. He whipped his head in that direction and saw nothing but grassy field and the edge of the barn. He shook his head in dismay and mounted his horse. All this talk of ghosts was getting to him, he decided, turning for home.

The rector and his wife stopped by the Judge's place several times over the next two weeks. Emily continued to fade, but her spirit was serene. She enjoyed their company and spoke of the good times they'd shared together. But she did not make any plans for the future; gently turning the conversation whenever someone tried to discuss what came next.

On the sixth week after the passing of the Judge, the rector was summoned again to the nearby village for a series of meetings on the mission effort. When the meetings were done, he drove back to Cambridge with Mr. Alden, a prominent citizen of the mission village who had business in town. The afternoon sun was shining brightly through the trees as they trotted down the road that led past the Judge's residence. They were a couple of miles from the Judge's gate when a black carriage drawn by a white horse came up rapidly from behind; sweeping past them and out of view. For some reason, the sight gave the rector chills. A white horse pulling a black carriage was too close for his liking to the ghostly description the Judge's daughter had given him.

"That fellow must be in a hurry to reach Cambridge," the rector said to cover his unease.

"There's something peculiar about that vehicle," Mr. Alden said. "It moves very quietly. I didn't hear it coming, and it made no sound as it went by. Not a rattle of wheels or the clop of a hoofbeat. It was very strange." He shuddered as he spoke and looked away from the road.

The rector turned the conversation to other topics, and soon the quiet carriage was forgotten.

They had driven another mile when the same white horse and black carriage appeared again, racing up silently from behind, squeezing past them in the narrow roadway and hurrying away at speed. There were no hoofbeats, no rumble of wheels or rattle of tack. The white horse and the black carriage materialized suddenly beside them and sped onward. There was no sign of the driver. The closed carriage curtains obscured him utterly save for his black-clad legs and boots.

"Where the blazes did he come from?" Mr. Alden cried in alarm. "There isn't a crossroad for miles! How did he get behind us again?"

"There was no noise," the rector commented, his hands shaking on the reins. "He was racing down the road at top speed, but there was no sound. I saw dust flying up from the wheels. We should have heard him coming!"

The rector felt sick to his stomach. There is no such thing as a death omen, he told himself firmly. There was some other explanation for this sudden appearance.

"That was the Judge's white horse," Mr. Alden said abruptly, pressing himself against the back of the seat. "I recognized it just now. It has one dark spot over its right eye that is unmistakable. I've seen the Judge drive that horse hundreds of times over the years."

The two men fell silent, too spooked by this second encounter to discuss it further. Their own horse and carriage rattled and bumped along noisily as they drove the next half mile. The sounds seemed magnified to the rector's ears after the silence of the black carriage.

They were within sight of the Judge's gate when the ghostly white horse and the black carriage came racing past their vehicle for the third time at high speed. A wave of cold air rushed over them as the carriage materialized next to them, white horse straining at the lines as it ran at full gallop down the road. The black carriage swayed and shook as it silently passed them; throwing up dust in its wake. Ahead of them, the carriage slewed sideways as it turned into the Judge's gate.

The rector gasped and urged his horse to a canter, only slowing as they themselves reached the gate just a few yards behind the other driver. The two men peered up the long lane toward the Judge's house. The white horse and black carriage were nowhere to be seen, nor were there any wheel tracks to mark their passing.

THE WHITE HORSE

"Dear God in Heaven," Mr. Alden said. "What do you think it means?"

"I'm not sure," the rector replied, shaken to the core. "Maybe he just drove behind the barn."

Neither man believed this explanation, but they let it stand as they trotted the remaining miles into Cambridge.

After dropping Mr. Alden off at his inn, the rector turned the carriage toward his home. He wondered, as he retraced his path beside the Judge's residence, if he should stop in and check on the family. On the one hand, he didn't want to alarm them further with tales of mysterious black carriages. On the other hand, he was their rector, and if they were in need he should be there.

The rector's musings were interrupted by a flash of white that blazed through the twilight. The Judge's gate was just ahead. The view was much more open from this direction, and he clearly saw the white horse pulling the black carriage down the lane from the house. The carriage curtains were still drawn, but he could see two pairs of feet now where there had been only one before. Beside the man's black trousers and boots were a lady's ruffled pink skirts and dainty shoes. The carriage turned silently into the lane ahead of the rector and sped off into the sunset. The rector shivered at the sight, realizing that it was exactly thirty days since the white horse had died in the Judge's front pasture.

"Goodbye, Emily," he said and turned his own vehicle into the Judge's gate, knowing the Judge's daughter and grandson would need their minister's presence in this sad hour.

19

Eavesdropper

HAGERSTOWN

This was, he told himself as he carefully set the long ladder against the side of the barn, *probably one of the stupidest things he had ever done.* The ladder thumped against the wall below the hayloft window with a soft thud, and the legs of the ladder slipped a bit on the snowy ground. He steadied the ladder and then blew on his bare hands to warm them.

The snow had come as a surprise that Christmas Eve morning, falling just long enough to coat the ground. He blamed the snow for the argument he'd had with his wife that afternoon. Miranda had started singing songs about white Christmases and had chattered about Christmas traditions and folktales. He hadn't minded her sudden zealous talk about the holiday until she mentioned her favorite legend.

"And they say," Miranda had said as she tied a ribbon around a gift for his mother, "that at midnight on Christmas Eve, the cattle kneel in the barn and speak to one another."

He had gaped at her incredulously and then had started laughing as he turned back to hang another ornament on the Christmas tree. Miranda had flushed and snapped: "It's true!

My Mama told me she heard them herself one Christmas Eve when she went to the barn to check on a sick heifer."

In retrospect, he probably shouldn't have called her mother a lunatic. That was a mistake Miranda would not soon forgive. They had argued for nearly an hour, forgetting the present wrapping and tree trimming. Then they had each gone away to sulk and were still rather cold with each other when they gathered again for dinner.

Miranda had taken herself to bed early with a headache. He had gone to bed an hour later and had lain beside his wife fuming about the silly argument. Finally, he had crept out of bed, careful not to wake her, had dressed in warm clothes, and come out to the barn. He wasn't sure what his motive was. Did he want to prove that Miranda was wrong, or that he was? He just knew he wouldn't be able to sleep until he'd seen for himself whether or not the cattle spoke at midnight on Christmas Eve.

Outside, he pulled the ladder out of the shed and carried it to the barn so that he could sneak up on his cows. According to the tale Miranda had spun, the cows did not appreciate eavesdroppers on their holiday conversation. When—as a young girl—Miranda's mother had arrived unexpectedly at the barn at midnight and heard the cows speaking to one another, she'd slipped into an empty stall to listen. But an unexpected sneeze had betrayed her presence, and the animals had stopped talking immediately when they heard her. Nary a word was spoken the whole time she was examining the sick heifer, and talk did not resume until she had exited the barn. Though Miranda's mother had stood for several minutes with her ear pressed to the door, she could not make out what the animals said.

He crept up the ladder as silently as he could, feeling foolish as all get-out for hiding from his own cows, and slipped through the open window. The hayloft was fragrant with the smell of dusty hay and sweaty cow. Thankfully, it was warmer in the loft than outside. He blew on his hands again and then lay down on the rough gray boards next to a fairly large knot-hole directly over the cow stalls and covered himself with hay to keep warm.

After waiting for what seemed like more than an hour, he grew drowsy and irritated, wanting his cozy bed and an unbroken night's sleep. It had to be after midnight, he thought, glancing at his wrist. To his chagrin, he realized that he'd left his watch in the house. He frowned and sat up. And then froze.

Below him, the cows started to low, one after another. He lay back down and pressed his eye to the knot-hole. One by one, the cows knelt in their stalls, and he saw his horse do the same. And within their soft calling he could make out real words. At first he could not understand more than a word or two here and there. Then he heard the cow underneath his hiding place say to its neighbor: "I am afraid our poor master will not live out the year."

"Oh, dear," exclaimed the neighboring cow. "What a pity."

He covered his mouth to prevent himself from gasping aloud. What were they saying? That he was going to die? He was in perfect health! His pulse started pounding, and he broke out in a cold sweat. No! He must be dreaming. He'd fallen asleep under the warm hay and dreamed the cows below him were speaking to each other.

"What will poor Miranda do without him?" he heard another cow ask as he jumped to his feet and hurried over to the window. He didn't care if this was a dream or not, he wanted to

EAVESDROPPER

get away from the barn as fast as he could. He slipped through the window, his feet fumbling for the first rung of the ladder. And then his sweating fingers slipped on the sill, and he felt his body falling toward the ground. He twisted desperately, trying to grab onto the ladder. Then he smashed headfirst into the icy ground. A brilliant flash of light went right through his head and he felt his neck snap. The world went dark.

Miranda went looking for her missing husband the next morning and found him dead beside the barn. The ladder to the hayloft window told her the rest of the story.

After word got around about the tragedy, people in those parts never again tried to eavesdrop on the talking cattle at midnight on Christmas Eve.

20

The Devil's Racecourse

BALTIMORE

Well, now, ol' Lucifer—the one we call the Devil—used to hang around these parts many years ago. There was one clearing I knew about at the outskirts of the city that had a huge burnt-out dirt circle in it. The circle was half an acre in size with a giant withered tree stump at the center. Nothing would grow in that circle, and no critter would set foot in it. Folks thought the Devil himself had made it, and no one went near it if they could possibly avoid it.

The Devil was a frequent visitor to Baltimore in those days, hanging about in the local taverns and trying to trick men into selling him their souls. There was one sailor—an ugly chap named Surly Bill—who he'd trapped into just such a contract, and the Devil tracked him down to his house when the man didn't live up to his end of their bargain. But the sailor was a clever fellow and had had a couple of priests come in to bless his house. The Devil couldn't go near the sailor's property, so he stomped off to the burnt-out circle in the clearing at the edge of town to sulk. As he sat upon the withered stump at its center, he spotted Sam Jones on his way home after work.

Now Sam was a freed slave who was too poor to buy a posh house in town. All he could afford was a little cottage that was far too close to the burnt-out circle for poor Sam's comfort, and he tried to get home before dark each night for fear of what he might see in the neighboring field. But on that particular day, Sam's last errand had ended on the far side of Baltimore, and it was dusk by the time he reached the path leading past the clearing. It was on this path, only a few hundred yards from his cottage door, that Sam met the Devil.

"I know you, Sam Jones," said the Devil in a tone whose deep, resonating edges raised the hair on the back of Sam's neck. "You are a fine, churchgoing fellow and a credit to your family." The Devil contrived to make this statement sound like a serious character flaw.

Sam blinked warily up at the dark, shrouded figure looming over him. All of his instincts were screaming at him to bolt for his door as fast as his legs would carry him, but he was frozen to the spot.

"I want you to take this letter to Surly Bill's house," the Devil continued. Sam gulped, unable to speak as the Devil thrust a letter into one of his hands and a coin in the other. Sam yelped and almost dropped the coin, which was so hot that its edges were glowing red.

"Go now, Sam!" the Devil ordered. The paralysis that had trapped Sam Jones fell away, and the poor man ran for his life, back down the path toward the center of town and the house where Surly Bill lived. Sam made the trip in record time. At his timid knock, Surly Bill whipped the door open and shouted: "What the devil do you want?"

"A letter for you, sir," Sam gasped, thrusting it into his hand and fleeing back into the dark night without so much as asking for a tip.

Surly Bill stood for a long moment, staring down at the seal on the back of the letter. Into the red wax was stamped the horned head of the Devil. The tiny eyes twinkled for a moment up at him and then went flat again. Surly Bill gulped, closed the door, and carried the letter back to his fire.

He'd been drunk the night he'd made his contract with the Devil and couldn't remember much of the encounter. Now, he read all the particulars of the deal as the fire died down to coals and his supper, stewing in a black cauldron, grew cold.

Surly Bill had promised to deliver another man's soul into the Devil's keeping in exchange for riches and good fortune for five years. It had to be the soul of a wicked man, it had to be delivered to the Devil within the next two months, and Surly Bill had to shed the man's blood with his own two hands in order to fulfill the contract.

Surly Bill's mind whirled as he considered the letter. He was not a good man, and he had no qualms about murdering someone. Indeed, he had done so before, having served for many years under a pirate captain who had captured more than fifty ships, killing their crews mercilessly as he robbed them of their cargo. Now the chest of gold Surly Bill had brought with him when he settled in Baltimore was almost empty. If he made good on his contract with the Devil, he would have more gold then he could carry, and else beside.

Surly Bill reviewed the wicked chaps he had known, but in his heart he had already decided that it was his old captain whose life he would claim for the Devil. The pirate captain had once had him tied to the mainmast and flogged until ribbons of skin hung from his back for breaking into a liquor cask without permission. Surly Bill hated the captain for giving him this treatment, and he had left his ship permanently at the next port, which had been Baltimore. Now he could wreak vengeance upon the captain and earn great riches in one go.

Packing up his satchel, Surly Bill went down to the docks and hired onto a ship sailing to the Caribbean in search of his old captain and crew. The Devil must have been helping him along, for he found the pirate ship fairly quickly and shipped aboard with them. Biding his time, Surly Bill waited until they were anchored off-shore from an island before picking a private, late-night fight with his captain, cutting his throat and tipping the body overboard. Then he slipped into one of the tenders tied to the back of the ship and rowed himself to shore with the captain's personal sea chest. By dawn, Surly Bill had boarded another ship and was on his way to Europe with more money than he had ever dreamed of possessing.

For five delirious years Surly Bill roamed the capitals of Europe, reveling in riches, wine, and song. He chased women feverishly and tried to buy their affections, but in vain. He drank like a lord without ever once getting drunk, gamed fiercely and won every time, and flung his money around recklessly. Yet somehow, Surly Bill never won any friends. People were frightened by the wild look in his eyes and by the faint mark of a claw that appeared like a brand on his forehead whenever he got angry. He had first noticed the faint mark on the night he murdered the pirate captain, and as the five years of pleasure promised to him by the Devil drew to a close, the mark got darker and began to be visible all the time.

Plotting feverishly to buy more time from the Devil, Surly Bill sailed for home. He had once kept the Devil at bay by having the local priest bless his home, he thought; he should be able to contrive a similar plan now. Other men had fooled the Devil in the past, and Surly Bill was confident that he could do the same. When the Devil came knocking on his door at the end of the five years, Surly Bill would be ready for him!

As he made his way homeward from the docks on the last night of his five-year contract, a thick fog descended upon Baltimore. Surly Bill groped his way homeward, following streets that no longer seemed familiar. Ahead of him—always ahead of him—he saw bright lights and heard cheerful voices. He knew he must be getting close to the center of town, and from there he could find his way home. But the lights stayed just out of reach, and the cobbles under his feet somehow turned to dirt and stones and became a wooded pathway. Suddenly, the fog lifted, and Surly Bill found himself on the edge of a clearing with a huge burnt-out circle in its center. He gave a gasp and turned to run. And found himself face-to-face with the Devil.

A little farther down the path that skirted the edge of the clearing, Sam Jones was making his way home. He had taken to carrying a rifle after his first encounter with the Devil, and he always wore a cross around his neck and kept a vial of holy water in his pocket, just in case. As he followed unknowingly in Surly Bill's footsteps, Sam was overtaken by a mighty storm that lashed the trees until one fell with a mighty crash. The rain beat down on him, and the wind tried to force him off the path. Thunder rumbled, and lightning struck ahead of him, behind him. He saw a large rock shatter from the force of one sizzling bolt.

THE DEVIL'S RACECOURSE

Then, over the moaning wind, Sam Jones heard a terrible screaming sound coming from the burnt-out dirt clearing just up ahead of him. He stopped in his tracks as hail began to beat down on him, not sure if he should run to help the screamer or flee for his life. But Sam's Christian upbringing was stronger than his fear, and so he forced himself forward on wobbling legs to peer through a thicket into the clearing.

Running around and around the burnt-out dirt circle like a racehorse on a track was the tattered, wild-eyed figure of Surly Bill. He was thrashing his arms against the wind and rain, and he kept screaming dementedly about getting an extension to his contract. Surly Bill did not seem to realize he was racing around in circles. Loping behind him with a happy smile was the dark, flame-encased figure of the Devil. The pouring rain and hard hail did not touch him; it turned to steam several feet above his head. The Evil One seemed to be playing with the crazed man like a mouse plays with a cat.

As if sensing Sam's gaze, the Devil turned toward the thicket where he crouched in fear and winked. Sam reeled backward, dropping his rifle to clutch his cross in one hand and pull forth the bottle of holy water with the other. Before his terrified eyes, the heavens opened and a huge column of molten lava fell from the roiling thunderclouds, turning the entire circle into a burning, fiery pit. From the depths of the flames, Sam could hear the Devil laughing.

After spending the night under his bed, Sam crept out to the burnt-out circle in the clearing—which was ever-after called the Devil's racecourse—and found the charred head of Surly Bill grinning dementedly atop the tree stump at the center of the clearing. His body was never found.

21

Marmaduke Mister's Gold

SMITH ISLAND

Well now, my next-door neighbor—crazy ol' Marmaduke Mister—used to spend all his time walking around the island with a shovel. Seems his grandpappy told him that Blackbeard the pirate had buried treasure on Smith Island, and Marmaduke was determined to find it. Folks were always falling into holes that Marmaduke had dug for treasure, or they would find the grass ripped up in their backyard where that rascal had dug a pit and then tried to fill it back in so it wouldn't show.

One summer, a stranger came to the island hawking treasure maps. He told a wonderful story about his great-great-uncle, who was a trusted friend of Blackbeard. The uncle had been given a map containing the location of Blackbeard's treasure just before the pirate's fatal last voyage. The map had been handed down in the stranger's family, but alas, none of them had been able to "decipher its mysteries," and so the stranger—who had fallen on hard times—was willing to part with the map for the staggering price of two dollars (and a hot bowl of soup).

Well, the rest of us islanders sniggered at the notion of anyone selling a treasure map for two dollars, but Marmaduke listened with dropped jaw and gleaming eye. Here at last was his big break, and he aimed to take it. Rubbing his grimy hands together with glee, he pulled out two dollars and took the stranger home with him. Miz Mister made the fellow some lunch, and then the two crazy men went treasure huntin' with shovels over their shoulder. That was the last time any of us saw the stranger, and, oddly enough, it was also the last time we saw Marmaduke running around the island with a shovel.

A few weeks later, Marmaduke came around the docks wearing a fancy new shirt and trousers. This was a bit strange, but we didn't say much about it aside from the jokes we always tell when a feller gets some fancy new duds. We all wondered how he could afford them new clothes, since Marmaduke spent more time digging for treasure than tonging for oysters. We put it aside as a peculiar circumstance and headed out in the boats for the day's fishing.

But that was not the end of Marmaduke's purchases. He got a new hat and a new coat, and his missus came to church on Sunday in a new dress. A few weeks later, Marmaduke went out and asked the local shipbuilder to make him a shiny new skipjack. And he paid the man in gold!

Well, the next day at the docks, all the watermen surrounded Marmaduke Mister and demanded an explanation. All he would say is: "'Tis none of yer business! Leave a body alone!" Then he waved us away and climbed aboard his tattered old log canoe with his eldest boy, who was wearing a sharp new outfit that gleamed blue and white in the summer sun.

Best we could figure, Marmaduke must have found Blackbeard's treasure after all. We were agog to hear the story, and I was kicking myself mightily for not buying the map from the stranger. But no one in the Mister family—least of all Marmaduke—would say anything about their sudden wealth. They'd snub anyone who brought it up. Finally, the whole island became resigned to never knowin' the true story of the Misters' wealth. In the end, this didn't matter too much, since it allowed each of us to make up our own stories about the treasure without fear of being proved wrong by ol' Marmaduke. In fact, speculatin' about the Mister fortune became a favorite way of passing the long winter nights on the island, and the tales we created became quite far-fetched and legendary.

Well, life seemed like a bed of roses for the Mister family for a while, until their eldest son was swept overboard during a storm and never seen again. Then Miz Mister took sick and couldn't leave her bed even to use the privy. Their middle daughter got in the family way, and her young man was killed by a bolt of lightning before they could get hitched and set things straight. Round about then, Marmaduke injured his leg while cutting wood for the family stove and had to be rushed to the mainland to have it removed 'cause it went septic. Folks around here started saying that the pirate's treasure Marmaduke had found must have been cursed.

Marmaduke lost his sparkle after he lost his leg, and when Miz Mister died a few weeks later, all the fight went right out of him. A young member of the Mister family told me in confidence that his pap went out into the woods one evening carrying a heavy chest full of pirate gold and a shovel, and came back at sunrise empty-handed. Marmaduke died the next day. On his deathbed, he told his family this: "I ain't never going to tell you where I buried that cursed pirate gold, 'cause it'll only bring you more bad luck. And you tell them nosy old men down at the docks that if they try to find the gold, they won't never be able to get hold of it. It will slip right out of their hands and disappear."

The Mister children were impressed with their father's last words, and they passed the message along to us watermen as we sat around the dock swapping stories while we mended our equipment. None of the Mister kids tried to find that buried treasure, but you can be sure the rest of us took a look around for it when we thought no one was watching.

Living next door to crazy ol' Marmaduke had given me an edge on the treasure hunt, and I slipped out of my house around midnight a month to the day after the old man's death with a shovel over my shoulder. I'd never believed that the Mister family was under a curse—after all, many of the families on Smith Island had similar difficulties without finding so much as a piece of pirate gold to blame for it—so I figured finding that chest wouldn't hurt me none.

Me and Marmaduke had played together as lads, and we had a favorite old tree where we used to leave messages for each other. Sometimes we'd bury our boyhood treasures down by the roots. I was pretty sure that this was the place Marmaduke had buried his unlucky treasure chest.

The trees were bare in the chilly spring air, and the full moon cast shadows hither and yon as if it were daylight. The wind rustled through the bare branches and swirled dead leaves around my feet as I tramped toward the message tree. A breeze ruffled my hair and for a moment, I thought I caught the echo of a voice whisperin' in my ear: "Leave a body alone!" I shivered a bit and pulled my coat closer around me.

Once I was certain I hadn't been followed, I started digging among the roots of the message tree, and it wasn't long before my shovel hit something hard. As my shovel thudded against the wooden chest, I heard the voice again: "Leave a body alone!" it moaned. At that moment, the wind struck me so hard I stumbled and had to fight to stay upright. It died away as suddenly as it came, and I grit my teeth and kept digging.

Soon, I uncovered a small, battered chest. My heart was dancin' in my chest, I was that excited. Gold! Pirate gold! I dropped down on the roots of the message tree and reached into the hole to pull the treasure chest out. As my hands gripped the sides of the heavy box, the wind rose again, swirlin' around me like a tornado, and I heard Marmaduke's voice shouting: "Leave a body alone! Leave a body alone, I say!"

The voice came from behind me. I whipped around, clutching the box to my jacket, and saw the glowing white figure of ol' Marmaduke Mister with his fancy duds and his missing leg floating several feet off the ground, holdin' his shovel over his head with two hands like a sword. "Leave a body alone!" he shouted again as the wind pushed me from side to side. In my hands, the heavy chest began to slip downward, as if it were being tugged back into the dirt by unseen hands. I tried to hold onto it, but it seemed to become misty and see-through as it fell from my hands, and the chest vanished in a flash of light just before it hit the ground. Marmaduke's ghost and the whipping wind all disappeared with the box of treasure. When I turned back toward the tree, all signs of my digging—including my shovel—had also vanished.

Without a word, I took to my heels and ran all the way home. Maybe Marmaduke was right about the curse on the

MARMADUKE MISTER'S GOLD

pirate gold. Maybe not. But I was pretty sure he'd laid a curse of his own on that gold, and no one would ever be able to claim it again, just as he told his kids. I sure enough never tried to find it again.

22

The Hairy Toe

UPPER MARLBORO

Once there was an old woman who was out digging roots and picking herbs in the woods when she spotted something funny sticking out of the leaves. Taking a large stick, she dug and dug until she uncovered a great big hairy toe.

It was the largest toe she'd ever seen, and as fresh as if it had just been chopped off a giant's foot. *There's some real good meat on that toe*, the old woman thought. *It would make a real tasty dinner*. Scarcely believing her luck, the old woman put the toe in her basket with the herbs and roots and carried it home.

The old woman pulled out her big stew pot and put the hairy toe into the bottom with some vegetables and herbs. She boiled up a kettle-full of hairy toe soup, which she ate for dinner that night. And darned if it wasn't the best meal she'd had in weeks! The old woman went to bed that night with a full stomach and a big smile. It had been a very good day. Perhaps tomorrow she'd find another toe.

Along about midnight, a cold wind started blowing in the tops of the trees around the old woman's house. A large black cloud shaped like a giant's hand crept over the face of the full moon, and darkness fell over the world. And from somewhere in the trees there came a hollow voice, rumbling: "Hairy toe! Hairy toe! What happened to my hairy toe?"

In the house, the old woman stirred uneasily in her bed and pulled the covers up over her ears, as if she sensed something evil stalking through the woods around her cozy home.

Outside, there came a stomp-stomp-stomping noise as if a pair of very large feet was moving along the leaf-strewn path through the woods. The wind whistled and jerked at the treetops in the darkness and howled down the chimney of the cozy little house where the old woman slept. From the edge of the forest, a hollow voice with cavernous depths grumbled and rumbled through the night: "Hairy toe! Hairy toe! Where is my hairy toe?"

Dark clouds billowed before the cold wind, filling the sky until every last star disappeared as if it had never been. Silence fell over the woods and the meadows as all the night creatures fled before the stomp, stomp, stomping coming from the path. The night birds and critters shivered in their branches and burrows as a hollow voice howled: "Hairy toe, hairy toe! Where'd you put my hairy toe?"

Inside the house, the old woman snapped awake and stared up at the dark ceiling as the cold wind slammed the shutters again and again against the side of her house. Her whole body shook with fright as she listened to the angry howling coming from the edge of the woods.

Jumping out of bed, the old woman ran to the door, barred it, and then dragged the heavy kitchen table out to the hallway and pushed it against the portal. No strange monster could get through that! Satisfied that she was safe, the old woman went back to bed and lay down to sleep.

THE HAIRY TOE

Into the meadow outside the house came the stomp, stomp, stomping of giant feet crushing the tall grass and flowers. The wind swirled around and around, howling louder than a rushing train. From the maelstrom ripping apart the dark meadow, a hollow voice shrieked: "Hairy toe, Hairy toe! Give me back my hairy toe!"

The old woman cowered under her covers, shaking with fear. The wind slammed against the house so hard that all the boards shook, and then the front door of the cottage burst open with a bang, sending the kitchen table crashing across the floor and into the far wall. Then came the stomp, stomp, stomping noise of giant feet walking across the floorboards and up the stairs.

Peeping out from under the covers, the old woman saw a massive figure filling her doorway. Outside, the wind suddenly died away, leaving the woods and the meadows and the cottage in total silence. The giant figure in the doorway whispered: "Hairy toe, hairy toe. All's I want is my hairy toe."

The old woman sat bolt upright in bed and screamed in sheer terror: "I *ate* your hairy toe!"

And softly, so softly that no one but the old woman heard it, the giant figure replied: "I know."

No one living in the region ever saw the old woman again. The only clue to her disappearance was a giant footprint a neighbor found pressed deep into the loose soil of the meadow beside the house. The footprint was missing the left big toe.

They say that on nights when the moon is full and the wind whistles in the treetops, you can sometimes hear a hollow voice saying: "Now I've got my hairy toe."

23

Crooked Kate

SOMERSET COUNTY

Well, Tim Cramer was a good waterman—there can be no doubt on that score—but outside the trade he didn't have one lick of common sense. No sir, not one lick at all. Otherwise he wouldn't have taken on Crooked Kate the way he did on the wharf one day when he was unloading a couple baskets of hard jimmie crabs and a mess of fish from his skipjack.

Now everyone on the Eastern Shore knew Crooked Kate was a witch. When she got a bee in her bonnet about something, it was best to go along with whatever she wanted; otherwise, the worst sort of trouble would follow. But Tim Cramer was in a bad mood that day on account of a toothache, and when Crooked Kate swept up to him with her wild gray hair blowing in the wind and her wicked blue eyes sparkling in her gnarled old face, he ignored her completely. He didn't even say "Good morning!" or "How'd you do?" like any polite fellow would have done. He just kept on unloading his boat.

Crooked Kate wasn't used to being ignored. She swelled up like an indignant gander and said: "Tim Cramer, you give me that mess of fish you've got settin' in that basket."

"No," said Tim. He didn't even look up. Well, the shock on Crooked Kate's face was not a pleasant sight.

"Did you hear me, Tim Cramer?" she shrieked, enraged by his cavalier manner. "I want you to give me that mess of fish!"

"And I said 'no,'" Tim snapped. His tooth was aching something awful, and he just wanted to toddle home and lie down with a cool cloth over his face for the rest of the day. A confrontation with a witch didn't fit into these plans at all, so he was doing his best to ignore it.

"Tim Cramer, do you know who I am?" Crooked Kate said, drawing herself up as proudly as a duchess.

"I reckon I do," Tim snapped. "And I'm telling you plain that I have just enough fish in that basket for my dinner tonight. Now if it's crabs you're looking for, I've got an extra basketful right here."

Tim pulled up the second basket of jimmie crabs and plunked them down on the dock beside Crooked Kate. With a snarl of outrage, the haggard, gray-haired witch thrust her gnarled paw into the squirming pail of crabs, and they all dropped their claws immediately and flopped over dead.

Tim Cramer's jaw just about hit the dock in shock. Crooked Kate had just lost him half a day's wages!

"Why, you wicked old biddy! How dare you?" Tim shouted.

"You think this is bad?" sneered Crooked Kate, wrinkling up her wart-covered nose in derision. "Just you wait. By this time tomorrow, you'll be wishing you'd given me that mess of fish I asked for!"

She turned abruptly, her black cloak swirling about her like a thundercloud, and marched away. All the other watermen working at the pier that day shook their heads when they saw her walking away from Tim Cramer like that. Tim was in for some trouble, no doubt about it.

After this encounter, Tim's tooth was throbbing so bad he could barely stand up. He staggered over to his ol' mate Hank and asked him to sell his remaining basket of jimmies for him, since he needed to go home to bed. Then Tim lit out for home and spent the rest of the day laid out like a corpse on a cot in the kitchen, making his wife miserable with all his querulous demands. She begged him to go to the doctor to have his tooth removed, but Tim was completely against the notion. He didn't want no doctor poking around in his mouth, thank you.

About six o'clock, Tim's married daughter came rushing into their house in a panic. Her baby was sick with the croup and she wanted her ma to come over right quick to help him. Well, Tim found himself alone in the kitchen with nary a person to alleviate his suffering. Even worse, when he got up to take his next dose of the patent medicine they carried in the general store, he found that the bottle was empty. Groaning in pain and frustration, he got some money out of his wife's pocketbook and started out for the corner store, grumbling and moaning and clutching his sore jaw in a surfeit of self-pity.

Just then, who should come along but that old witch Crooked Kate.

She cackled when she saw Tim Cramer and muttered some strange-sounding words, waving her gnarled hands expressively toward him. Tim found himself falling to the ground, his arms lengthening so that suddenly he was standing on all fours. His body stretched and stretched, fore and aft, side to side, and when he tried to speak, all he could say was: "Hee-haw! Hee-haw!"

Tim jumped in shock and swished his tail. Then he jumped again, stunned by the fact that he now had a tail to swish, and started turning in circles, trying to look at himself. On the other side of the lane, Crooked Kate howled with laughter at the sight of a donkey chasing its tail in the center of the street. After a few dizzying seconds, Tim stopped whirling around and sat down in the dirt, braying his distress. The sight of a donkey sitting in the center of the street was nearly as funny as watching it chase its tail. Crooked Kate got a stitch in her side from laughing.

Tim Cramer was not amused. He hated being laughed at, and he did not care much for being a donkey either, although it seemed to have temporarily cured his toothache. He stood up on all four hooves, shook himself, and then tried to kick the wicked old woman from here to kingdom come. But Crooked Kate was ready for him. She dodged his flailing hind feet and nipped a magic bridle and bit into his mouth. Then she jumped up on the donkey's back and kicked him hard in the sides, pointing him down the road in the opposite direction from the general store.

Tim Cramer bucked and twisted his donkey's body, trying to throw off that old witch, but the magic bridle held him prisoner, and he was forced to run and jog and gallop and lope his way through miles and miles of brambles and briar bushes and soggy swampland, and as many other unpleasant places as the witch could find to ride him. Up and down the countryside they went, Crooked Kate cackling in triumph all the way.

"You'll give me some fish next time, Tim Cramer," she called over and over again, kicking the poor old donkey in the sides whenever he slowed his step.

Toward sunrise, Crooked Kate turned the donkey toward home. On the doorstep of the Cramer house, Crooked Kate removed the spell on Tim and left him gasping on the front porch, trembling and bleeding from hundreds of scratches. Missus Cramer came a-running when she heard them arrive and yelled a curse after the old witch when she saw the state her husband was in.

Missus Cramer called the doctor, and he bandaged poor Tim up good and proper and removed his sore tooth to boot. Tim stayed in bed for two whole days while the story of his humiliating transformation and hundred-mile ride swept up and down the Eastern Shore.

Tim was furious with the old witch and vowed to get even with her. Just as soon as he could stand up, he hobbled out to the kitchen and melted down a couple of his great-grandmama's silver spoons to make bullets. Then he drew a picture of Crooked Kate on a scrap of newspaper and hung it on his wall. Taking up his rifle, he loaded it with the silver bullets and shot the crude picture three times: once in the right leg, once in the stomach, and once in the neck.

Back in her cottage in the woods, Crooked Kate gave a sudden shriek of pain and keeled over dead, blood pouring from her body in several places. Scared the life out of a couple o' girls who'd come to the old witch for love potions to give to their unsuspecting beaux.

When the doctor was fetched, he found three gaping wounds on Crooked Kate's body—one on her neck, one across her stomach, and one in her right leg, with no explanation for how they got there.

CROOKED KATE

When the other witches who lived along the Eastern Shore heard about Crooked Kate's death, they knew what had happened, and they stopped pestering the local watermen for free food. So Tim Cramer did everyone a favor after all.

24

The Card Game

WARD'S CROSSING

THE CARD GAME

Well, now, Lloyd McCready was a steady man, a fine husband, and a good father. But even the finest fellows can have a flaw, and Lloyd's was gambling. He loved to play poker, and frankly, he wasn't any good at all. No sir! Lloyd always lost every round he played during the Saturday night games with the boys, and it was only on account of him being raised as a thrifty man by his granny that he didn't lose more than his weekly spending money at the cards.

Lloyd's wife, Matilda, was a saint if ever there was one. She worked evenings at the cannery, raised a passel of kids, and kept Lloyd on the straight-and-narrow road to heaven. But even she could not cure him of his gambling. Every Saturday come rain or shine, Lloyd would set off for Ward's Crossing and the local poker game.

"You'd best be careful, Lloyd McCready," Matilda said each Saturday evening before he left the house. "The Devil is in those cards!"

Lloyd just laughed, kissed his sweetheart of thirty-four years, and headed out the door. He was whistling to himself happily as he strolled up the road one evening in late autumn.

He passed the darkened confectionary stand where his enterprising young neighbor sold ice cream during the spring, summer, and early fall, noticing that the stand was carefully boarded up with a notice letting customers know that the stand would be opening again in the spring. Lloyd nodded approvingly. Billy Joe was a good lad. The confectionary stand was neat and clean, the benches and tables tucked away underneath—and the ditch where careless youngsters sometimes threw away their wrappers and what-not had even been cleaned out. It was a job well done, in Lloyd's opinion.

Lloyd continued on his way to Ward's Crossing and entered the home of Dan Gibson, one of his card-playing buddies. He was greeted with a shout, and his three friends started chanting a school cheer they'd learned in boyhood. Lloyd joined in heartily while Dan's wife and daughter rolled their eyes at such childish antics. After serving up a round of snacks, the women went over to a neighbor's house to drink tea and discuss the foibles of men.

Lloyd was in a cheerful mood that night. He wasn't much of a drinker, so he stuck to lemonade while his fellow card-addicts joked around and drank beer. To Lloyd's surprise, his first hand was a winner. He gave a loud yell of delight as he laid the hand down, saying: "This one's for me, lads!" It was a straight, and all the cards were spades.

Dan and the others grinned cheerfully, happy that their friend had won for once in his life. They passed around some cookies before dealing another round. A few minutes later,

Lloyd found himself staring at a flush, all spades. He blinked in astonishment, and then laid down a second winning hand, to the amazement of his fellow players. This was two more games than Lloyd had ever won in his entire life.

"This one's for t'missus, lads," Lloyd said, his face suddenly wreathed with a happy grin.

"Spades again, eh, Lloyd?" asked Dan as the others threw in their cards and Lloyd scooped up the pot.

"Coincidence, lads," Lloyd said, ignoring the sudden prickling sensation on his arms.

There was an intense silence when the next round was dealt, broken only by sounds of crunching as the men passed the molasses cookies around the table again. After a few moments, Lloyd found himself staring at a straight flush, all spades. He stared at his hand in shock. Another win? And with spades?

His granny had always referred to spades as the Devil's cards, and Lloyd suddenly remembered Matilda's weekly warning to him. The Devil was in the cards, she always said.

Lloyd shook his head slightly to clear it of these crazy thoughts and laid down his third winning hand of the night.

"This one's for the kiddies, lads," Lloyd said, his voice a little hoarse. The men stared in amazement at the cards. Then Dan stirred uneasily. "Spades," he said flatly.

"That's a lot of spades, Lloyd," Carl Taylor said in a strained voice that he tried to make jovial. "Sure you ain't cheating?"

They all laughed. Lloyd was such a terrible card player, he wouldn't know how to cheat if he'd wanted to.

"I don't like it," Dan muttered to himself as Lloyd scooped up the pot yet again. "My Mam always said spades were the Devil's cards."

Hearing his granny's words repeated aloud by Dan gave Lloyd the willies. Three lucky wins in a row—all spades—made him uneasy. *Superstitious rot*, he told himself, ignoring the goose bumps on his arms and settling himself down to another round of cards.

After a few minutes of play, Lloyd turned over one last card and found himself staring at a royal flush in spades. His stomach clenched, and he felt sweat rolling down his forehead, although his whole body felt cold.

"What have you got, Lloyd," Dan asked softly, his voice as tense as Lloyd felt. Lloyd carefully laid the cards down on the table. He heard his voice croak, as if from a distance, "And this one's for the Devil, lads."

The four men stared at the cards in awed silence.

"You win again, Lloyd," Dan said slowly, tossing down his cards. The others followed suit. No one could take their eyes off the royal flush of spades lying at the center of the card table.

"That's it for me," Carl Taylor said suddenly, his face white. "I've had enough cards for one night. Congratulations on your win, Lloyd."

The other men leapt up hurriedly, as if they were afraid the Devil was after them. The winning money was pushed unceremoniously into Lloyd's hands, and Dan's house cleared out with amazing speed. Lloyd's hat and jacket were produced, and he was escorted outside rather forcibly by Dan.

Lloyd found himself walking down the road toward home, his pockets full of money and his thoughts in a whirl. Then he rounded the corner and, to his astonishment, saw a red glow ahead of him where Billy Joe's concession stand stood.

Immediately, all thoughts of the strange card game left him as he took in the situation. Someone was trespassing on Billy Joe's property, and that someone was going to be real sorry in another moment if he'd harmed anything. Pulling out the .22 revolver he always carried, Lloyd moved cautiously along the shadowy road, his eyes fixed on the red glow.

As he drew nearer, he saw the light was flickering like flames from a large bonfire, and he could hear a clank and a rattle, as if the person trespassing were wearing chains. It looked as if the blaze had been set in the ditch, and Lloyd crept carefully off the road to investigate.

Reaching the edge of the ditch, Lloyd looked down and saw a ring of fire around the edges of the ditch. Seated within the ring were four men playing cards. Three of them were glowing a ghostly blue, and their bodies were translucent. Around their legs they wore heavy shackles, and the chains rattled and clinked whenever they moved. The fourth figure had a thin, evil face with glowing red-black eyes, a sharp goatee, a wicked grin, and small horns sticking up from his head. A glowing-red pitchfork hovered beside him as he lay down his cards in triumph.

It was a royal flush of spades.

"This one's for the Devil, lads," Lucifer said to his three prisoners. And as he spoke, he looked straight toward the clump of bushes where Lloyd stood frozen in shock.

Lloyd gave a shout of sheer terror and dropped his .22. He took to his heels and ran the rest of the way home, his pockets jingling and rattling with all the money he'd won playing cards that night. Lloyd flung himself into the house and slammed the door behind him. Matilda came running at once to see what was wrong. Leaning his back against the door and panting heavily,

THE CARD GAME

Lloyd managed to gasp out the entire story to his frightened wife.

"I told you," Matilda howled, almost in hysterics. "I told you the Devil was in the cards! You'd better give that money to the preacher right now before the Devil comes for it!"

Lloyd nodded, too weary to speak, and Matilda got on her coat and marched her erring husband right down the road to the preacher's house. She pounded on the door until the preacher came running in his nightclothes, and told him Lloyd's story. Then she thrust Lloyd's winnings into the preacher's startled hands and took her husband home.

The next morning, Lloyd and Matilda went down to the concession stand to look for his revolver. Shaking tooth and nail, Lloyd forced himself to peer down into the ditch where he'd seen the Devil the night before. At the bottom of the ditch lay a pack of cards. The cards were torn into what looked like a thousand pieces, save for the ten, jack, queen, king, and ace of spades, which lay facing upward at the very center of the ditch. Burned across the bottom corner of each card in the royal flush was the blackened print of a clawed thumb.

Lloyd gave a shout of terror and ran for home, followed by his wife. The McCreadys sent for the preacher and asked him to clean out the ditch by the concession stand and pray over the defiled grounds. When the preacher came to their home to return Lloyd's missing .22, he reported the concession stand free of the Devil and his minions.

But neither Lloyd nor Matilda could bring themselves to purchase any more ice cream from Billy Joe's shop, and Lloyd never played cards again.

25

Dawn's Early Light

FORT MCHENRY, BALTIMORE

It was the story of the Star Spangled Banner that drew me to Fort McHenry that hot summer day. I'd read a reference in a magazine to Francis Scott Key, the man who wrote the words to the Star Spangled Banner, and it had struck a chord with me. Anxious to learn more, I had looked up the history of our national anthem and its author.

During the War of 1812, Francis Scott Key, a young lawyer working in Washington, D.C., visited the British fleet occupying the Chesapeake Bay in an effort to secure the release of a Maryland doctor who had been abducted by the British. While Key's negotiations with the British had a successful outcome, their timing had been poor. Key and the doctor found themselves parked aboard a flag-of-truce sloop while the British fleet prepared to attack Baltimore and Fort McHenry, which guarded the entrance to the city's harbor.

The commander of Fort McHenry during this inauspicious occasion was Major George Armistead. About a year before the attack, the Major had commissioned Mary Young Pickersgill, a Baltimore widow who had experience making ship flags, to make the fort a huge United States flag measuring thirty by forty-two feet that would be clearly visible to the British, even from a distance.

With the help of her daughter Caroline, Mrs. Pickersgill spent several weeks creating the fifteen stars and fifteen stripes that would make up the flag, the future Star Spangled Banner. Their house was not large enough to do the final piecing, and so the flag was assembled by candlelight on the floor of a nearby brewery over the course of several evenings. Mrs. Pickersgill was paid $405.90 for the completed flag, which was presented to Major Armistead in August 1813.

On the morning of September 13, 1814, the battle for Baltimore—at the time an important international seaport with more than 50,000 residents—began. The British fleet, consisting of nineteen ships, began pounding the fort with rockets and high-trajectory mortar shells. After an initial exchange of fire, the British fleet withdrew to a point just beyond the range of Fort McHenry's cannons and continued to bombard the fort for the next twenty-five hours, firing between 1,500 and 1,800 rounds at the beleaguered fort, which was valiantly defended by a thousand dedicated American soldiers.

The battle raged all day during a terrible rainstorm. Thunder crashed, lightning struck, and the wind howled around the valiant soldiers manning the cannons in the fort. Francis Scott Key and the freed doctor had watched and listened anxiously throughout a very long, dark night from their position on the flag-of-truce sloop, which lay to anchor a good eight miles downstream from the fort. They heard only an occasional blast of return fire from the fort, and they feared the worst when the British bombardment tapered off toward morning.

By dawn's early light, Key grabbed a telescope, placed it to his eye, and looked toward the fort. Training the scope on the flagpole, his anxious gaze was met with the sight of Armistead's huge American flag flapping in the early morning breeze. The garrison flag had been raised as a gesture of defiance toward the British, replacing the sodden storm flag that had flown throughout the battle-stricken night.

Heady with relief at the thrilling sight, Francis Scott Key pulled a letter from his pocket and jotted down a few lines of verse on the envelope:

O say, can you see, by the dawn's early light,
What so proudly we hailed at the twilight's last gleaming,
Whose broad stripes and bright stars, through the perilous fight,
O'er the ramparts we watched, were so gallantly streaming?
And the rockets' red glare, the bombs bursting in air,
Gave proof through the night that our flag was still there;
O say, does that star-spangled banner yet wave
O'er the land of the free and the home of the brave?

When the defeated British fleet had withdrawn, Key and the doctor continued on to Baltimore. Key completed his poem in a Baltimore hotel and sent it—under the title of *The Defense of Fort McHenry*—to a printer for duplication on handbills. The poem was popular from the start and was (ironically) set to the tune of a British drinking song called "To Anacreon in Heaven." Both song and flag quickly became known as "The Star-Spangled Banner," and the song was made the United States' national anthem by a Congressional resolution on March 3, 1931. I was fascinated to learn that there were actually four versus to the poem, since I had only ever heard one, and I had taken the time to memorize the entire song before my visit to Fort McHenry.

After parking my car in the lot, I paused for a moment to peer up at the statue of Major George Armistead opposite the Visitor Center before going inside to learn more about the fort. Its construction began in 1799 and was completed in 1802. Fort McHenry was built in the shape of a star with five bastions, following a popular century-old French design. Each point of the star was visible from the points on either side, so that every area of land surrounding the fort could be covered by as few as five men. Impressive! At the time of the Battle of Baltimore, the fort had four barracks, a powder house, and a guardhouse that stood next to the commanding officer's barracks.

I wandered out into the morning sunlight, blinking in the sudden brightness as I squinted toward the star-shaped fort and the huge flag waving gallantly above it in the soft breeze. The grass glowed a brilliant, heady green as I strolled along the sidewalk, looking out over the river harbor at the ships and trying to picture the British fleet floating just out of reach of the fort's cannons. On the morning of September 18, 1814, that huge fleet must have seemed dire and threatening to the one thousand brave soldiers watching from these shores. But on the 19th, by dawn's early light, things had changed dramatically. Perhaps Key said it best, in the second verse of the national anthem:

On the shore, dimly seen thro' the mist of the deep,
Where the foe's haughty host in dread silence reposes,
What is that which the breeze, o'er the towering steep,
As it fitfully blows, half conceals, half discloses?

Now it catches the gleam of the morning's first beam,
In full glory reflected, now shines on the stream
'Tis the star-spangled banner. Oh! long may it wave
O'er the land of the free and the home of the brave!

As I approached the fort, I saw a raised mound on my right that—according to the pamphlets I had dutifully picked up at the Visitor Center—was the remains of the dry moat that originally encircled the fort and protected many of its defenders during the bombardment. A V-shaped outwork opposite the fort entrance was called a ravelin, and its purpose was to protect the entrance from direct attack. The underground magazine into which I peered was added after the Battle of Baltimore.

I climbed up onto the ravelin, again trying to picture the scene on the day of the battle, but it was hard to do with the sun sparkling on the water and a huge barge anchored off to one side. I sighed and then scampered down to the bottom like a little kid. Feeling mischievous, I circled the outside of the fort once, following a footpath around the moat and examining the Civil War batteries, all the time thinking about the third verse of Key's poem. Key had taunted the vanquished British, who had disappeared so completely from this place that it would be difficult for people like me to imagine the battle scene nearly two hundred years later.

And where is that band who so vauntingly swore
That the havoc of war and the battle's confusion
A home and a country should leave us no more?
Their blood has washed out their foul footstep's pollution.

No refuge could save the hireling and slave
From the terror of flight, or the gloom of the grave,
And the star-spangled banner in triumph doth wave
O'er the land of the free and the home of the brave.

There was an archway over the sally port through which I entered the fort. According to my reading, this was constructed after the battle. I paused and bent down to look into some underground rooms on either side of the entrance that were originally bomb proofs. Then I entered the parade ground, and found myself—between one moment and the next—stepping into the past. Suddenly, I stood in the darkness of night with the roar of cannon and the shrieking sound of incoming shells competing with growling thunder. I was instantly soaked to the skin by a heavy downpour, and my eyes were dazzled as flashes of lightning vied with the brilliant flashes of the battery firing from the bay.

I stood staring at the scene, confused and petrified with fear. Where was I? What had happened? A sudden, devastating crash on my right nearly knocked me down as a bomb tore through the powder magazine. Fortunately, it was a dud, or the whole Fort would have been blown to kingdom come. A grimy, soaking-wet soldier stopped suddenly in his race toward the damaged building and called out to me: "Miss, you shouldn't be out here! It's too dangerous. Get back to the supply lines!"

I gaped at him and then turned tail and ran back through the entrance and out of the embattled fort. As I fled, the rain about me lessened and the dark sky slowly brightened with dawn's early light, as if each step I took moved the battle forward toward its conclusion. I raced in the direction where

I knew the Visitor Center must lie—although apparently not in this time—past the ravelin and out over the moat, and then stopped dead. The bay was filled from end to end by the British fleet—bomb ships, frigates, and one rocket vessel loomed on the near horizon. But I saw immediately that they had ceased firing, and some were already sailing back down the river.

Light was filling the sky. I turned slowly and lifted my gaze above the ramparts, and through the mist, I saw the flag. The Star Spangled Banner was rising up the pole as I watched. It was already gallantly streaming in the morning breeze by the time it reached the top, and I stood with tears in my eyes as the light of the long-ago dawn gradually became the brilliant noon-day light of the present. The flag I now saw was a re-creation of the original, which was preserved in the Smithsonian Museum in Washington, D.C.

I took a deep breath, shaken by all that I had just experienced. Retrocognition—the psychic ability to know something about a situation after its occurrence—was not unknown in my family, which could trace its lineage back to some of the most controversial witches and hex doctors along the East Coast. But like many psychic events, retrocognition usually caught the viewer unaware, as my current vision had. I gave another shuddering sigh, drawing looks of concern from several passing visitors, though no one ventured a comment.

Finding a bench, I sat down awhile to calm my nerves. As I did, the last verse of Francis Scott Key's poem flashed through my mind.

O thus be it ever when free-men shall stand
Between their lov'd home and the war's desolation;

DAWN'S EARLY LIGHT

Blest with vict'ry and peace, may the heav'n-rescued land
Praise the Pow'r that hath made and preserv'd us a nation!
Then conquer we must, when our cause it is just,
And this be our motto: "In God is our trust!"
And the star-spangled banner in triumph shall wave
O'er the land of the free and the home of the brave!

According to the information in the Visitor Center, it is a tradition that when a new flag is designed for use by the United States, it is first flown over Fort McHenry—over the very same ramparts where I had seen a flag gleaming in the aftermath of a terrible battle. I nodded to myself thoughtfully. Yes, that was appropriate. Where else should the first official flags with forty-nine and then fifty stars have flown but here? Here, where they could greet the dawn's early light and triumphantly express the unity and strength that stand between our beloved home and war's desolation.

Rising slowly from the bench, I placed my right hand over my heart, just as I had been taught at school when I was a child, and bowed slightly to the flapping flag shining brilliantly in the sun.

"'Tis the star-spangled banner," I said aloud. "Oh! long may you wave, o'er the land of the free and the home of the brave!"

Then I made my way back toward my car and pointed it homeward.

26

Heartbeat

ELLICOTT CITY

Something was going on. Jason felt it in his bones. Polly was too happy, too cheerful all the time. No woman could be that upbeat and still be faithful to her husband; of this he was morally certain.

It maddened Jason that he could never catch Polly flirting with another man, or even talking with one on the phone. She stayed near him at parties and local charity events, and they sat together holding hands each Sunday morning at church. All their friends and neighbors thought they were completely devoted to one another. But he knew better!

Polly had married beneath her class, of course. Her parents had always hated him. They still joked about how she gave up marrying her high school sweetheart—who became a lawyer—to marry him. Polly thought they were kidding, but Jason knew they weren't. He'd seen the sideways glances they threw at him when she wasn't looking, and they still had Polly's prom photo—*with the other man*—up on the living room wall.

Jason sat down to a delicious, warm meal every night—that couldn't be right—and Polly sang to herself as she washed up afterward. What kind of woman could be cheerful doing dishes, unless she was sure that in the near future she would never wash a plate again? As Jason read the newspaper after dinner, he would listen to her chatting on the phone with her mother or one of the church ladies. Strain as he might, Jason never heard anything that hinted of a secret romance. It drove him crazy. Life was not this perfect. It couldn't be. There was a flaw somewhere, and he was determined to find it.

Maybe Polly was seeing the milkman, or the greengrocer. Jason started getting up early in order to see who it was that delivered the milk. Much to his disappointment, the fellow that creaked up to their front door looked as if he'd been born several centuries ago and had kept living out of sheer stubbornness. The remains of his white hair were thin and greasy, he had so many wrinkles it was hard to tell where his eyes were, and he stooped over so low that he had to drop his hand only a few inches to place the bottles on the doorstep. Just in case, he asked the old man his name. Joe Smith. Ha! Obviously an alias. Still, he looked a bit too creaky to be courting a beautiful, classy lady like Polly.

Jason started doing the food shopping, and checked out every single male employee in the local grocery store. They were either antediluvian relicts—like the milkman—or still in diapers. None seemed the type to sweep his wife off her feet. Jason grumbled to himself as he stomped home. Polly met him at the door with a kiss, and she'd made a plate full of his favorite cookies while he was gone, just to thank him for doing the shopping. Yes, there was definitely something going on!

In mid-September, his father-in-law called and jovially asked if Jason would like to help fix up his old car. He agreed at once, rather pleased the old man thought so well of his abilities. They joked around as they poked and prodded at the old car, sliding under it skillfully like a couple of grease monkeys.

Jason was working underneath the car when he heard his father-in-law call: "Hiya, Hank!"

Hank was the name of Polly's high-school boyfriend. Jason rolled out from under the car and quickly stood up.

"Hello, Mr. Parker." A tall, handsome young man had come to the entrance of the driveway to shake hands.

Jason's father-in-law beamed. "It's nice to see you! How are Helen and the kids?"

"Fine, just fine," Hank said with a smile.

"Say, have you met my son-in-law? This is Polly's husband, Jason. They just got married about this time last year, isn't that right, son?" his father-in-law said, pulling him forward and introducing the two men. Jason gripped Hank's hand so hard the lawyer blanched a bit, and massaged it behind his back once they dropped the clinch.

"Hank and his family just moved back to town," his father-in-law continued, oblivious to the rage shaking his son-in-law. "You joined Ted Mallory's firm, right?"

Hank nodded and elaborated on the topic for several minutes before continuing on his way. Jason kept his cool and went back to working on the car as if there were nothing wrong. But inside he was triumphant. Now he knew! He knew why Polly was so happy all the time. Her parents must have told her that Hank was coming home, and she was planning on running off with him. Jason disregarded the notion that Hank would remain faithful to his wife and children after meeting Polly again. Why would he want someone else if he could have Polly?

Enraged with jealousy, he was waiting in the kitchen when Polly got back from her church meeting and began roaring out his anger as soon as she shut the door.

"What are you talking about?" Polly yelled when he paused for breath. "Why would I want to be with anyone else but you? I love you!"

But Jason was beyond reason. He snatched up a newly sharpened steak knife, howling: "You've cut out my heart, now I'll cut out yours!" He leapt around the table toward his cowering wife and ripped her still-beating heart out of her chest with the knife. Blood streaming everywhere, he sailed out the back door into the dark night and flung her heart, still thumping warmly against his hand, over the side of the bridge that spanned the creek next to their home and into the swirling water beneath.

He cleaned up the blood-stained house with extreme care and buried Polly's body deep in the woods outside of town. Then he wrote several letters, carefully mimicking Polly's handwriting, and mailed them to himself and her parents. Within a few days, everyone in town believed that Polly had been secretly seeing a man from the next town that she'd met through her charity work, and that they had run away together. Polly's parents were heartbroken and apologized again and again to Jason for their daughter's cruelty. Jason was careful to play the role of a grieved and betrayed husband. And he *had* been betrayed—he was convinced of it in his soul. He knew that Polly had decided to get back together with that lawyer, even though it hadn't actually happened yet.

He went out to the bridge later that evening and watched the dark water swirling around in satisfaction. Polly had gotten what she deserved, he thought. As he breathed in the night air, he became aware of a vibration under his feet.

Da-dum. Da-dum. Da-dum.

The sound was so faint that Jason could barely hear it at first. It floated softly through the air, a rhythmic thudding that trapped everything else in its beat.

Da-dum. Da-dum. Da-dum.

Jason's hands began to tingle as he recognized the soft thudding sound. It was the same beat he had felt when he held Polly's bleeding heart in his hands as he ran from their house to this bridge.

Da-dum. Da-dum. Da-dum.

The heartbeat grew louder as he stood frozen beside the railing of the bridge.

Da-dum. Da-dum. Da-dum.

The heartbeat rang in his ears, thundering so loud that he was afraid it would wake the neighbors.

"No!" Jason shouted. "No, Polly! No!"

He clapped his hands over his ears and ran back to the house, slamming the door against the terrible, relentless beat that pulsed from underneath the bridge. He couldn't hear the sound in the kitchen, but the floorboards seemed to vibrate slightly under his feet to a slow, steady rhythm. He fled into the living room and picked up the newspaper, trying to regain some semblance of normalcy by returning to his nightly routine.

Da-dum. Da-dum. Da-dum.

He gradually became aware that the words in the article he was reading were following a faint, rhythmic pattern that ebbed and flowed around a soft, steady beat.

Da-dum. Da-dum. Da-dum.

HEARTBEAT

It sounded like a heartbeat.

Da-dum. Da-dum. Da-dum.

Polly's heartbeat.

Da-dum. Da-dum. Da-dum.

Jason screamed in terror and flung himself out of the house, running toward the bridge as the heartbeat grew louder and louder in his ears.

"Curse you, Polly! Curse you," he shouted dementedly.

Lights went on in the neighboring houses as Jason leaned over the railing where he had flung Polly's beating heart.

"Curse you!" he shouted, as his next-door neighbor tried to pull him off the rail. Jason yanked away from him impatiently, intent on reaching the heart—that horrible, betraying heart—and silencing it forever. He could hear nothing of his neighbors' frantic cries or the women screaming. Nothing save the dreadful heartbeat.

Da-dum. Da-dum. Da-dum.

With a wild shriek, Jason flung himself headfirst off the bridge like a diver. The neighbors all heard the very final crunching sound of his head hitting the rocks below, and the snap of a breaking neck.

There was a stunned silence. Then, the gathered neighbors became aware of a very faint vibration coming up through the soles of their feet: *Da-dum. Da-dum. Da-dum.*

It felt like the slow, steady beat of a human heart.

27

Jack O'Lantern

WORCHESTER COUNTY

I thought I'd do some hunting in the marshlands on my day off. Much to my disgust, I didn't shoot a thing all day, and come sundown I was simmering with frustration. I'd wandered pretty deep into the bogs and swamps, and before I knew it dark was falling and I was a long, long walk from where I'd stashed my car. Worse still, I was a bit turned around. I was pretty sure I knew the way back, but what with the dusky twilight and the rising mist, I figured I had better hightail it out of there mighty quick.

At first, the walking wasn't too bad. I could still see the thin game trail I'd been following along the wobbly ground and through the treacherous tufts of grass. But the light was fading, and I hadn't brought a flashlight. Stupid of me. I clutched my rifle closer and kept moving forward slowly as the mist began to billow in strange shapes, swirling in a manner calculated to convert the greatest skeptic into a believer in ghosts.

I gulped a bit and kept going, until I almost fell headlong into a deep pool that loomed out of nowhere in the mist-shrouded darkness. I groped my way backward and sat down on a rotting log. It was no use going on tonight. If I did, I was sure to injure myself or fall into a pool of water and drown.

I shivered, already feeling the damp deep in my bones. It would be chilly tonight, but not cold enough to kill me, I figured—for which I was grateful. What a stupid mess to have gotten into, I fumed, trying to make myself comfortable on the ground beside the log. Around me, I could hear the soft whirring and croaking and singing of the night creatures, and the wind soughed through the tall grasses and trees. The mist was so heavy now I couldn't see my hand until it was right in front of my nose.

And then the first light appeared, off to my right. I was startled. Was there another hunter out here? Someone with a flashlight who could get me out of this pickle?

I jumped up and shouted: "Hello there!"

My voice reverberated in the foggy air, but there was no response. I sat down again, watching for another light. Nothing.

I sighed and lay down beside the log, determined to get some sleep. And then the light appeared again, off to my left this time. It winked on and off. On and off. Then disappeared. That was when I realized what it was. It was the Jack O'Lantern. A will-o'-the-wisp. These fairy lights, common to marshlands around the world, were said by some to belong to evil spirits who tried to lure the unwary to their doom. This was nonsense, of course. Science said the lights were caused by marsh gases.

I relaxed, grinning to myself as I recalled the quaint piece of folklore attached to the marsh lights. According to my great-uncle, Jack was a nasty fellow who beat his wife and kids and was an all-around bad chap. So the Devil came and hauled the poor fellow away with him. On their way to hell, Jack asked the Devil if he was thirsty, and ol' Lucifer said he was, so Jack somehow persuaded the Devil to turn himself into a coin so

Jack could buy them both a drink from a nearby tavern. Only Jack stuck the Devil into his coin purse, which had a cross on it, and wouldn't let the Devil out until he agreed to give Jack another twelve months of living. The Devil didn't have much choice in the matter unless he wanted to live forever in a satchel, so he agreed and Jack let him out.

Jack went back to his wicked ways, figuring he'd repent and get religion during the second half of his stolen year, and that would be good enough to keep the Devil away. Only Jack kept putting off the time when he'd change his ways, until one day he opened the door and found the Devil on his threshold. Away went Jack and the Devil, going down to hell. When they passed a great big tree full of apples, Jack asked the Devil if they could get some of the fruit for a snack to eat on their way to perdition. The Devil agreed, so Jack gave the Devil a lift into the branches so he could pick them some fruit. Once the Devil was up the tree, Jack whipped out his jackknife and carved a cross in the bark so that he couldn't come down.

"Lemme down," shouted the Devil, but Jack wouldn't let him down until the Devil promised to never come after him no more. Then Jack rubbed out the cross carved into the bark until you couldn't see it, and the Devil was free. The Devil stomped off without another word, and Jack could do as he pleased from then on.

Well, Jack got worse and worse as the years rolled by. But all good things must come to an end, and Jack's body finally got so wore out that he died. Jack's spirit went straight to the gates of heaven, but Saint Peter refused to let such a wretched fellow in, and Jack was forced to go down to hell. But the Devil barred the door as soon as he saw Jack coming and wouldn't let him in to hell either. "Go away and don't come back," the Devil told Jack. "Go back where you came from."

"How am I supposed to get back in the dark?" Jack grumbled. "Give me a lantern."

The Devil threw a chunk of molten fire out to Jack, who took it for his lantern and went back to earth, where he wanders forever through the swamps and marshlands of the earth, a bitter spirit whose only delight was in luring the unwary to their doom with his lamp.

Anyhow, that's the story my great-uncle told me when I was a kid.

"Is that you, Jack O'Lantern?" I called jovially the next time I saw the light.

"Jack, (jack, jack)," a voice whispered back at me from the fog. I was seriously spooked. I clutched my gun to my chest, the hairs on my arms standing on end. Had that been an echo of my voice, or was someone out here with me?

"Who's there?" I shouted, trying to sound brave and menacing. I waved my gun around. "Show yourself."

"Jack, (jack, jack)," the voice hissed from a completely different section of the swamp. A light blinked on and then off. On and then off.

Shudders ran up my spine at the sound of that ghastly voice coming from nowhere. I huddled up against the log, wanting something firm at my back. Suddenly, the story of the Jack O'Lantern didn't seem so funny. After all, this was a man who had outwitted the Devil, and whose bitterness at being cast out of both heaven and hell caused him to lure the unwary to their deaths. Nonsense and hokum, of course. But it didn't seem like it here in the chill dark with the wind whispering through the grass and the fog obscuring everything from view except a strange, blinking light that wouldn't stay put.

My heart was pounding so hard it made my chest hurt. I strained my ears in the silence that fell over the swamp. I couldn't hear anything; no croaking frogs, no buzzing insects, no swish of owl wings. The silence was uncanny.

"Jack, (jack, jack)," the voice hissed, from somewhere to my left this time. The light blinked on, off, on . . . I counted ten heartbeats this time before it went out. The voice sounded closer. I held very still, my instincts screaming at me to hold my breath and not move until the menace had passed. Time enough tomorrow to laugh at my foolishness if this was just some hunter's prank. For now, best to stay safe, huddled with my back against the rotting log, the smell of the swamp stinging my nose.

The voice came again, far off to the right.

"Jack, (jack, jack)," it hissed. The light came on, off, on . . . off.

It's moving away, I thought, relaxing just a bit. Feeling safer.

There was a long, long, long silence. Nothing stirred, not the wind in the grass, not the frogs or turtles in the water, not the crickets or night insects. Not even a bat on the wing.

"Jack, (jack, jack)," the voice hissed softly, right into my ear. And I looked up into the glowing red eyes and twisted face of the Jack O'Lantern.

I screamed and lashed out at it with my gun, and ran a few steps. I tripped and fell over, knocking my head on a sharp stone. For a moment I saw stars, and I felt blood pouring from my scalp. But the Jack O'Lantern was right behind me, and my only thought was to get away. I rolled and fell into the deep

JACK O'LANTERN

pool that had almost trapped me before. I plunged underneath the water, flailing desperately against ropelike grasses that tried to keep me down. My head finally burst out of the water, and I gasped desperately for air, treading water as best I could with my trembling limbs and aching head. I heard the creature laugh in the mist.

"Jack, (jack, jack)," the voice hissed delightedly, and the light blinked on, off, on right over my head, blinding my dazed eyes as horror flowed through me and froze my limbs so I could no longer swim. For a long moment, the grotesque face and red eyes of the Jack O'Lantern loomed out of the mist before my petrified gaze.

My head started to swim with pain and my cut bled more freely. The evil face above me, lit by its bright light, whirled around and around, growing dimmer as my eyes started to glaze. I was vaguely aware that I should keep swimming, keep trying to make my way to the edge of the pool, but the effort was too much for my suddenly heavy limbs. I barely noticed myself plunging down and down into the watery depths of the pool, too stunned by my injury to fight my way to the surface a second time.

Then there was only darkness, and silence, and a voice hissing in cold triumph: "Jack, (jack, jack)."

28

Der Belznickel

ST. MARY'S COUNTY

My sisters and my baby brother danced about the house, whispering to each other excitedly about the coming of der Belznickel on that snowy December 5th evening, the day before the Feast of Saint Nicholas. According to the stories, the good Saint Nicholas chains up the Devil on the eve of his birthday—December 6th—and makes him visit all of the children in the village to see if they have been behaving themselves and deserved the attention of *Kirstkindel.* Those who are good will receive gifts, but those who are naughty . . . well, those children who do not know their prayers or their school recitations or who have been troublesome at home might find themselves whipped with der Belznickel's switch or tied up with his chains, and they will receive coal in their stockings instead of presents.

Of course, I did not participate in the excited whispering or silly romping of the youngsters. I was above such foolishness, having turned twelve on my last birthday. Instead, I peeled potatoes in the kitchen to help *meine Muter* with dinner. I heard several pairs of feet stampeding up the stairs and shaking the floorboards over my head, and I sighed a little at all the dramatics. Just then, someone tugged on my skirt, and I looked down at Hans, my three-year-old brother.

"Gretel, will der Belznickel come tonight?" he asked me, his huge blue eyes wide with anxiety. I scooped him up into my arms and gave him a reassuring hug.

"Yes, Hans, he will come tonight," I told him.

And he would too. I had seen Uncle Oskar stashing a dark costume—consisting of raggedy fur-trimmed black clothes, a headband with goat-horns glued to the top, a long whippy switch, and a thick, rattling chain—in the empty stall in the barn about an hour before sunset.

Right after dinner, Uncle Oskar would duck out to "see to the horses," and a few moments later, der Belznickel would make his visit to see if we children had been good enough to receive the attentions of Saint Nicholas tomorrow.

"Will he have a switch and chains? Will he tie us up?" Hans asked.

"Der Belznickel only ties up naughty little boys and girls. But you have been good, so you need not worry," I said. Hans still looked a bit uncertain.

"Were you ever tied up, Gretel?" he asked, fingering my long blond braid nervously.

"Never. I am always *ein gutes Mädchen*—a good girl," I said a bit smugly. "Der Belznickel will ask us to recite our lessons from school and then will give us some sugar candy."

"Inga said he chased her up and down the hallway last year, rattling his chain," Hans said.

"That's because he found out Inga cheated on her spelling test at school," I said. "She almost got coal in her stocking instead of presents, except she said she was sorry to Muter and

Vater, and that made der Belznickel leave her alone. But you've been very good this year, and so has Inga. There won't be any chasing; just recitations and candy."

This reassured Hans. I put him down and he scampered off upstairs to talk to Inga and my other sisters while I finished the potatoes.

There were fourteen of us at dinner that night—Muter, Vater, my four sisters and three brothers, Uncle Oskar, Aunt Helga, their two children, and me. As the oldest child, I watched over the others and made sure that the babies got fed. Then Uncle Oskar slipped out to "feed the horses" and the grown-ups exchanged happy grins over the little children's heads.

The first sign that "der Belznickel" was approaching was a loud, rude banging on the front windows. Hans and Inga screamed when a soot-covered face with long black whiskers was pressed against the glass. Then the front door burst opened and der Belznickel rumbled into the parlor, rattling his chains. The children cowered and whimpered and screamed half in fear and half in delight at the raggedy creature with his goat's horns and bag full of something—was it candy or coal? The answer depended on what happened next!

Der Belznickel made all of us—even me—line up in a row in our parlor. Starting with me, we began to answer whatever questions he asked us. He rattled his switch at me and made me quote the Scripture passage from last Sunday's church service. Martin—the next oldest—recited a poem he had memorized for school. And so on down the line. Every time we got an answer right, der Belznickel would stomp about in rage because he hadn't tricked us, and the little ones would squeal.

I was distracted from Uncle Oskar's antics by a strange flickering in the lantern light. Something was wrong with Uncle Oskar's shadow. I began watching it as he made Ludwig recite next. When Uncle Oskar lunged one way, the shadow went the opposite way. As I watched, it lifted the chains over its head. The shadow's hands seemed impossibly long, and the fingers looked more like claws. I shivered, chills running over my skin. The horns on the shadow's head were very sharp, and the legs too long. Then the shadow broke away from Uncle Oskar completely, just as Ludwig finished his recitation. As the grown-ups and children all cheered for Ludwig's success, the shadow slid over the wall like oil and coiled up near the ceiling. Then it opened its glowing yellow eyes and looked straight at me.

I gasped, my heart pounding and my legs shaking. My terror was masked by the happy shrieks of the youngest children, who were watching Uncle Oskar—the pretend Belznickel—stomping up and down the hallway rattling his chains and howling in "anger."

I faced the opposite direction, toward the corner of the room, watching the real Belznickel slide down the wall, his shadowy form slowly solidifying into a short, twisted figure dressed in coal-black fur with a broken nose and vibrant yellow eyes. No one else noticed him as he slithered like a snake past my parents and Aunt Helga and began stalking the hallway at Uncle Oskar's heels.

My stomach was twisted into a knot. I wanted to run away and be sick, but I couldn't tear my eyes off the evil figure that stopped before my cousins and watched as they spelled several difficult words at Uncle Oskar's request. Johanna stumbled a bit, and der Belznickel gave an audible chuckle and seemed to grow larger within the shadow of my uncle Oskar. When Johanna recovered herself enough to finish spelling her word successfully, der Belznickel shrunk in size and frowned. Occasionally, the creature would dart a look at me and give me a twisted grin.

Little Hans was the last one in line, and he was terrified. He stared up at large Uncle Oskar and couldn't breathe a word.

"Have you been a good boy?" Uncle Oskar asked, taking pity on the small figure. Hans nodded fervently, and Uncle Oskar patted his head and handed him a boiled sweet. Behind him, der Belznickel stomped in rage and then dematerialized, becoming a thick black oozing mass that gradually sank back into Uncle Oskar's shadow and disappeared.

I staggered a little, as if a weight had been released from me, and stared suspiciously at the shadow, wondering if the creature was really gone for good. My siblings and cousins were mobbing Uncle Oskar, demanding sweets from "der Belznickel" since they had all done so well with their recitations.

As he handed out the treats, I heard a knock at the window. I looked out into a pair of glowing yellow eyes in a twisted face.

"I will see you again next year, Gretel," der Belznickel hissed through the glass. "Try not to be too good."

I screamed then and fainted, toppling to the floor before my Vater could catch me. They told me later that all was confusion in the parlor for several minutes, during which time Uncle Oskar slipped away. I awoke to the stinging sensation of smelling salts, and clung to my Muter and cried as if I were no older than Hans. My siblings and cousins laughed at me, their own fear forgotten, but my Muter hushed them, realizing that my terror had nothing to do with Uncle Oskar. She sent them away to the kitchen to eat their sweets. When they were gone, I told Muter and Vater and Aunt Helga what I had seen and heard.

Vater nodded his head several times as I spoke, and then said: "*Meine Kind*, I once saw the real der Belznickel too when I was about your age. I will tell you now what my Vater told me then. Der Belznickel is bound by the goodness of Saint Nicholas. If you are a good child—if you do your best and try to be kind and say your prayers—no harm will come to you."

I shuddered, remembering the look on der Belznickel's face when he called my name.

"I will, Vater. I will," I promised fervently.

"I have heard that people who see der Belznickel also have the good fortune to see Saint Nicholas," Aunt Helga added unexpectedly. "My Muter told me that she saw them both at the Feast the year she turned twelve. Watch carefully tomorrow, Gretel, and you may also see the blessed Saint."

The grown-ups hustled me to bed after that, and Muter tucked me up tight. I was quickly joined by my sisters, who drifted off immediately, but I couldn't sleep. I kept seeing the leering face of der Belznickel before me and hearing him call my name. Downstairs, the grandfather clock chimed the hours away as the house grew quiet and the adults went to bed.

As time ticked its way toward midnight, a moonbeam shone through the window, shining across the room and dazzling my eyes. Beautiful, it was, and comforting. I slipped out of bed and went to look out at the moon that was turning our room into a shadowy and mysterious place. It was as bright as noon outside, and the trees and bushes cast serene shadows over the snowy landscape. Then I saw, riding up to the road on a dashing white horse, a bearded man dressed in red with white fur lining his

DER BELZNICKEL

hood. It was Saint Nicholas. Running before him and muttering darkly was der Belznickel. The grim little figure seemed more comic than scary now, bound by his rattling chains and forced to dance to the whim of the good Saint behind him.

For a moment, the Saint paused in front of my house and looked up at my window. He raised a solemn hand to me, and I smiled and waved back. Then he spurred his horse away down the road, der Belznickel scampering ahead of him like a little black dog, and they disappeared into the dazzling snowscape under the light of the full moon.

With a soft sigh, I returned to the comfort of my bed, sensing that this was the last time I would see either der Belznickel or Saint Nicholas. And I knew something else too. I knew that I had nothing to fear from the grim little creature, not now, not ever. I fell asleep with a smile on my face and woke the next morning to the joyful shouts of my siblings on Saint Nicholas Day.

29

Black Aggie

PIKESVILLE

Yes, it's true I was once a watchman for the Druid Ridge Cemetery in Pikesville, although that was many years ago now. I had been on the cemetery staff for a number of years when the famous Civil War General and publisher of the *Baltimore American*—Felix Agnus—put up the life-sized shrouded bronze statue of a grieving angel, seated on a pedestal, in the Agnus family plot just before his mother passed away.

Some sort of scandal erupted over the statue about a year after it was erected in the cemetery. It turned out that this "original" sculpture was actually the copy of a piece commissioned by Henry Adams, grandson of President John Quincy Adams, as a memorial to his wife. Agnus was given a lot of grief about the statue, but he hung on to it and later on he, and then his wife, were buried in its shadow.

The statue was eerie by day, showing a figure frozen in a moment of grief and terrible pain. At night, the figure was almost unbelievably creepy, the shroud over its head obscuring the face until you were up close to it. There was a living air about the grieving angel, as if its arms could really reach out and grab you if you weren't careful. The Agnus plot was not my favorite place to walk after dark once that statue appeared.

I had often wondered if statues or houses or even people were changed when they were named, taking on something of the character of the name they received. After seeing the Agnus statue—which bore the nickname "Grief"—I came to the conclusion that this was true.

When doing my nighttime rounds, I had noticed that some parts of the cemetery had an almost luminous quality, even on nights without a moon, as if some type of blessing lingered over the ground. Other parts seemed quiet and peaceful, as if the people lying there just wanted to rest throughout eternity. But the Agnus plot was different. With the arrival of the dark angel, a sense of anger and malice seemed to fill the area. It was not a sorrowful grief represented by the statue. The grief it characterized was the angry, vengeful grief that will not forgive, that stalks those who have brought about such a terrible pain. Such were my musings as I made my nightly rounds. Even when the moon was full, the area around the statue remained dark, as if the silvery light could not touch the place where the grieving angel sat and brooded in her bitter anger.

Slowly, I came to dread the time when I walked past the statue. It felt as if a storm were brewing in that part of the cemetery, and I did not particularly want to be there when it broke. I began to notice, on the very darkest nights, at the time of the new moon, that gray shadows seemed to cluster near the statue; strange, shimmering wisps that may or may not have been ghosts and dark spirits. I've seen a ghost or two in my time, having inherited the Second Sight from my mother, and these were not the gentle beings I had glimpsed in the past. I refused to walk alone in the graveyard on those nights.

I suppose I shouldn't have been surprised when the stories began. I was not the only person who noticed the dark atmosphere surrounding the statue. Folks visiting the cemetery after dark were often spooked at the sight of it. I began to hear rumors that the statue—nicknamed Black Aggie—was haunted by the spirit of a mistreated wife who lay beneath her feet. I laughed aloud when my children told me that story. But the tales continued and grew more bizarre.

I heard many reports of the statue's power. According to local gossip, the statue's eyes would glow red at the stroke of midnight, and any living person who returned the statue's gaze would instantly be struck blind. Any pregnant woman who passed through her shadow would miscarry. If you sat on her lap at night, the statue would come to life and crush you to death in her dark embrace. If you spoke Black Aggie's name three times at midnight in front of a dark mirror, the evil angel would appear and pull you down to hell. They also said that spirits of the dead would rise from their graves on dark nights to gather around the statue. (Well, okay, I couldn't discount *this* story, as I had seen something similar happen myself during my nighttime rounds. Probably the dark atmosphere surrounding the Agnus plot attracted them.)

People began visiting the cemetery just to see the statue, which made my watchman's job much more difficult; especially when people came in the middle of the night or when they tried to deface the statue in some way. Then a local fraternity began making the statue of Grief part of their initiation rites. "Black Aggie" sitting, whereby candidates for membership had to spend the night crouched beneath the statue with their backs to the grave of General Agnus, became popular. Once we heard about that, the cemetery had to hire additional watchmen to chase away the nocturnal visitors.

A new story began to circulate about that time. According to the college students, one of us watchmen heard a scream on the stroke of midnight and hurried to the Agnus plot, only to discover the body of a young man lying at the foot of the statue. The young man had apparently died of fright. I would have laughed at that story if I'd found anything about Black Aggie laughable by that time. The statue was more of a pain in the neck than a menace to me now. I was nearing retirement, and so was reluctant to give up my job, but sometimes the Black Aggie legend got to me.

Well, the years passed—far too quickly—and the time came for me to retire. I was on night duty again during that final month of my career, and I spent much of my time running off Black Aggie thrill seekers. But on my very last Thursday, the cemetery was strangely quiet and bereft of visitors. It was one of those silvery, moonlit nights where everything seems magical and luminous, and I strolled through the night feeling as light as air. Even the approach to the Agnus plot did not seem as dark and menacing as before, and I had almost forgotten about the grieving angel until I came right up to it. It was midnight, or close enough to it as to make no difference, and as I drew near to the statue, it stirred. I stopped dead in complete astonishment, my arms pricking with a sudden superstitious fear. The shrouded head turned toward me, and I saw the gleam of glowing red eyes beneath the concealing hood.

Right up until that moment, I had always discounted the stories I'd heard about Black Aggie, although I had known from the start that there was something dark about the grieving statue. My flashlight dropped from my nerveless fingers, but my legs were frozen to the spot, and I couldn't run. The air around me was filled with a darkness that slowly blotted out the silvery moonlight, and a sense of twisted grief and anger pulsed through the night.

Words flashed into my head as I felt the dark angel's pain, and I spoke them aloud: "You were named Grief, not Anger, nor Vengeance. Sleep now, grieving angel, and grieve no more." Then I spoke a few Latin phrases my grandmother had taught me when I was small and frightened by nightmares—*Exorcizo te, immunde spiritus, in nomine Patris et Filii, et Spiritus Sancti, ut exeas, et recedas ab hac famula Dei.* These words would help drive away the Devil or his minions should they try to harm me. The Latin had always seemed meaningless to me, until that night. But in the darkness of the Agnus plot, the words seemed to boom with a hidden power, and the shrouded figure slowly resumed its seat as I spoke them, the red glow fading from its eyes.

Gradually, the silvery moonlight returned, filling the whole area and driving away the shadows. I groped around on the ground for my flashlight, my eyes never leaving the statue. Had I imagined the whole thing? Were there college students hiding behind the statue even now, laughing silently at the trick they had just played on the old watchman? I didn't stay to find out.

My last night on the job passed without incident—after we drove off a carload of Black Aggie hunters—and I left the cemetery at dawn without looking back. I heard later that one of the angel's arms was cut off one night and found later in the trunk of a car. The car's owner claimed that Black Aggie had cut

BLACK AGGIE

off her own arm in a fit of grief and had given it to him, but the judge sent him to jail nonetheless.

The disruption caused by the statue grew so acute that the Agnus family finally donated it to the Smithsonian museum in Washington, D.C., where it sat for many years in storage. So the Druid Hill Park Cemetery lost its grieving angel, which was all for the best. But sometimes I still wonder about the statue called Black Aggie. Was it really haunted? Or was the whole thing just a crazy story?

30

The Floating Coffin

HOOPERS ISLAND

'Twas a sad day when they lowered the coffin of my missus into the hard ground. I've been a tough waterman all my days, but I confess I wept like a young 'un. Living on an island where the water table is high, we don't bury our loved ones underground. So my wife was placed in a fancy monument in the local graveyard after the preacher said some comforting words.

The other watermen said I wasn't myself after my missus passed and I knew they were right. Her death knocked the stuffing clean out of me. She was my first and only sweetheart. She'd had a wicked sense of humor and was a great cook. And she was smart enough to rescue me when I made a mess of things, which happened more often than I care to admit. Without her sparkling presence in the cabin, I felt every one of my seventy-plus years.

I still went out on the boats at sunrise, fishing, crabbing, and oystering like I'd done my whole life. I'd never wanted to retire. My dad never retired and I didn't see the point, up until now. But the sights and smells of the water, the jokes and sly asides of my comrades, didn't lift my heart the way they used to. After my wife passed, I spent many hours staring out at the sparkling sun on the bay, feeling tired and old.

There were signs of bad weather a-coming that August of 1933. A big hurricane was rolling up the coast, aiming right for us. Some folks left the island to stay with their family on the mainland. I knew my kids wanted me to come, but I couldn't summon the energy to leave my cabin. So I hunkered down as the rain pounded the tin roof with the force of gunshots and the wind shook the cabin in mighty gusts. It was a humdinger of a storm. The waves rose higher and higher until they licked my doorstep. And that's when I realized that I'd been a fool to stay on the island. I probably wasn't going to make it out of this situation alive.

"I messed up again, Tilly," I muttered as I gathered up my wife's Bible and a few other prized possessions and climbed to the second-floor bedroom just ahead of the storm surge. "I reckon I'll be joining you shortly."

Downstairs, water flowed into the cabin through every crack and crevice. The cabin was built to last, and it resisted the steady pounding of the mighty waves. But the water crept higher and higher. I couldn't swim, so when it reached me, it would be all over.

I'd retreated onto the bed by the upstairs window as water rose up the staircase and spread over the floor of the second story. I was reading the Bible in the poor storm light, preparing to meet my Maker, when I heard a funny tapping sound at the window beside me. Between the roar of the storm and the metallic rattling of rain on the tin roof, I'd almost missed it. But each time a wave swelled against the cabin, I heard the noise again. *Tap-tap.* A pause as the wave receded. *Tap-tap.* The sound came again with the next wave.

I peered through the rain-slicked glass, but twilight had come early with the storm, and I had no idea what was making the noise. It was a big window, and the bottom sill was already underwater. It was a stupid idea to open the window and look outside. But Tilly would be the first to tell you that I do stupid real well. So I dropped into the water beside the bed and pulled up on the bottom pane of the window as the latest swell died away. I looked outside but still didn't see much of anything. Then I was knocked clean off my feet by a huge wooden box that swept through the cabin window with the next wave. I sat sputtering in a foot of salty water and rubbed my eyes, not believing what I saw. A ding-dang-dong coffin was bobbing next to the bed. What the blazes? I pulled myself upright using the bed blankets as the wind drove more rain and water through the window. Why was there a floating coffin in my bedroom?

I shivered in my suddenly soaked clothes and crawled along the top of the bed until I could read the name burned into the top panel. Matilda Smith. I gasped in shock. That was my wife's name. Surely not! I reached out two shaking hands and pulled up the lid. I looked down at the peaceful face of my Tilly. There was a little smile on those lips, as if she were trying not to laugh. She always looked like that when she was getting me out of a mess of my own making. Her body was surprisingly well preserved for all the weeks she'd been gone. She looked as if she was just sleeping.

I lowered the lid and stared at the little package beside me. It contained my most precious possessions, and it was as waterproof as I could make it. I thrust Tilly's Bible inside the

THE FLOATING COFFIN

bundle and then put everything into the coffin with my wife. I sealed the lid and shoved the coffin out the second-floor window. Grabbing a decorative oar from the wall, I climbed aboard my makeshift boat and floated off into the storm.

The next few hours were pretty much a blur of cold rain, sloshing waves, and misery. I don't know how long I clung to the top of the coffin, rowing and steering as best I could; making for higher ground on an adjacent island. Suddenly, the coffin bumped into dry land, and I heard voices exclaiming in horror. Many hands pulled me ashore, and I knew I was safe.

"The coffin," I gasped to the men who rescued me. "Get the coffin. It's my wife!"

A few of the younger lads waded in and pulled the walnut box to safety. I broke away from them for a moment and fell against it. "Thanks, Tilly," I panted. "You got me out of another mess." I lifted the lid and retrieved my belongings. Then the crowd lifted me up and away to warmth, light, dry clothes, and steaming hot food. I was safe.

Most folks don't believe me when I tell them the story of the floating coffin. But I swear on Tilly's Bible that every word is true. The doctors tell me I've got at least another decade to enjoy my grandkids, and it's all thanks to Tilly.

31

Buried Alive

EASTON

It was a cold autumn. I wasn't surprised when Mama, who had a weak constitution, caught a chill. She became quite ill, and nothing the doctor did seemed to help. After several nights of restlessness and high fever, she suddenly grew cold and stopped breathing. I was stricken when I brought her lunch upstairs and found that she was gone.

We were all heartbroken—Papa most of all. It was a cold, windy day in November when family, friends, and servants gathered in the garden to lay poor Mama to rest. I wept bitterly and could not be comforted. On the other side of the open grave the family butler hovered, glaring bitterly at Papa. My father's sturdy frame shook with grief as the minister spoke the eulogy. He didn't notice the butler's anger, but I did. The butler wasn't upset about Mama's death. No, he was angry over some slight one of the family members had given him that morning. To me, it was a trifling thing compared with the tragic death of our mother, but he could not forget it.

Later I heard the butler in the kitchen, complaining to the cook about all the valuable jewelry that had been buried with my mother. "First they insult me, and then they waste all that money on a dead woman," he said loudly.

"Hush," the cook said, nervously glancing about. "The Master will not tolerate such talk."

"The Master! The Master!" the butler said, his face turning beet red. "I'll tell you what I think of the Master." He started swearing then, using words I'd never heard before and didn't care to know the meaning of. I clapped my hands over my ears and hurried away, shocked at such behavior.

As my maid prepared me for bed that night, I saw a light flashing in the garden. Curious, I glanced outside and saw the butler stalking down the garden toward the family graveyard carrying a lantern. The sight made me uneasy. *He must be on an errand for Papa,* I thought. But my skin prickled as I remembered his words in the kitchen.

Instead of going to bed, I made my way downstairs and mentioned what I'd seen to one of the footmen and to the cook, who was washing up the last of the dishes. "I'm sure he's doing something for your Papa," Cook said reassuringly. "He was just talking nonsense before to relieve his feelings. I wouldn't worry about it, my dear."

Somewhat reassured, I hurried upstairs. As I silently passed Papa's study, I caught a glimpse of him through the open door. He was standing in front of a roaring fire, his face sad. I knocked on the doorframe. When Papa looked up, I hurried in to give him a comforting hug. Outside, the wind picked up and I caught a glimpse of snowflakes piling up against the window. I shivered, imagining my poor cold mother buried under the snow. Tears poured down my cheeks and I buried my face against Papa's shoulder as I wept.

After leaving the study, I paused on the landing and glanced out the window to see if I could spot the butler going about his errand for Papa. I still felt terribly uneasy, in spite of Cook's words. I glimpsed a faint light glowing in the family graveyard and thought for a moment that I heard a shout of alarm. But it may have only been the wind gusting against the house as the snow began falling in earnest.

I went to bed but couldn't sleep. After tossing and turning for nearly an hour, I rose, dressed, and went down to the kitchen for a drink of water. Cook was still there, sitting in front of the fire with her cup. She smiled when she saw me, a sympathetic smile. She knew how close I'd been to my mother. Her compassionate look brought the tears again, and she held me close and let me weep until the rush of pain had passed. Then she made me drink a hot cup of tea.

As I swallowed my tea, I heard someone knock at the kitchen door. Cook looked surprised.

"Who could that be at this time of night?" she muttered. She hustled across the room and opened the door. Then she screamed so loud that she woke the whole house. I heard thumps upstairs as people leapt out of their beds, and voices exclaimed in surprise. I ran toward Cook to see what was wrong. And saw my mother kneeling in the snow by the kitchen door, cradling a bleeding hand.

"It's a ghost! The mistress has returned as a ghost," Cook wailed.

I reeled backward in horror at the sight. Why had Mother returned as a ghost?

A crowd of servants had descended upon the kitchen, summoned by Cook's scream. At the sight of my mother's ghost, they too screamed, gasping and wringing their hands.

I stood frozen in my bathrobe and slippers, unable to move, my eyes taking in the grisly spectacle. Mama knelt on the stoop, pale as a ghost. Behind her, I could see a trail of blood leading back toward the graveyard. That didn't make sense. *Do corpses bleed?* I wondered. I didn't think they did. That's when I realized the truth. "Oh dear God," I cried. "We buried her alive!"

I flung myself toward my kneeling mother and the servants pulled me back, afraid of what the phantom might do to me.

Papa arrived, thrusting his way through masses. He gasped when he saw Mama on the stoop.

"Martha!" he shouted, breaking the spell of horror that had overtaken all of us. Papa leapt into the snow and pulled Mother's body inside. "She's breathing," he cried a moment later. "She's alive! Quickly, someone, summon the doctor. And get blankets to warm her. Build up the fire."

A living woman was a far cry from a ghostly haunting. Papa was overwhelmed by servants rushing about trying to make themselves useful.

"Dear God, what happened to her hand?" Papa asked, trying to mop up the blood with his handkerchief.

I hung back, still unnerved by the sight of my living mother after I'd seen her buried earlier in the day. There was a bloody stump where one of her fingers had been cut off. That finger had borne an expensive ruby ring when she was buried. I noticed that all the jewelry had been stripped from her body. I shivered suddenly, all the little clues slowly coming together in my shocked mind.

The kitchen door was still open, and I looked out at the snowy ground and once again saw the trail of blood, rapidly being covered by snowflakes.

"How did Mama get out of the coffin?" I asked suddenly. "It was buried under the ground."

Papa's head jerked up. He stared at me, mouth agape. The whole kitchen went still.

"And where's all her jewelry? She had a ruby ring on the finger that is missing."

"We'd best find out," Papa said, suddenly grim. He tenderly handed Mama to her lady's maid and stalked out the door with several footmen. I borrowed Cook's shawl and followed. I was convinced the butler was behind all this. But he'd probably already run away.

We followed the faint trail of blood in the snow. The marks indicated that Mama had walked—no, had crawled—from the graveyard to the door.

Ahead of me, I heard my father swearing and the footmen exclaiming in horror. I skidded up beside them and looked down on a six-foot hole in the ground. The coffin gaped open, but it wasn't empty. Inside lay the butler, facedown. He wasn't moving. A shovel and a spilled sack full of my mother's jewelry sat at the edge of the hole. The lantern lay extinguished on its side in the new-fallen snow

"Lying, smirking thief!" My father was still shouting.

"But Master, it was probably the shock of the cut finger that woke her up," one of the footmen said cautiously. "She must have sprung up suddenly and scared the butler half to death. Look at the marks in the snow! Here's where the Mistress sprang up and out of the tomb. And these are the butler's footprints. He tried to run away, but he slipped right here and fell into the grave instead. He must have knocked himself out when he fell, otherwise he'd be long gone by now."

BURIED ALIVE

My father stopped in mid-sputter. The footman was right.

"Wake him up and get him out of there," Papa said finally. "We will take him to the constable, though I will probably not prosecute him as thoroughly as he deserves."

The footmen slid cautiously into the hole. Then one yelped: "He's dead! Master, he's dead!"

They hoisted the body up, and we realized the butler had landed on his own knife when he fell into the coffin. Which seemed a fitting end.

The doctor reattached Mama's finger and made her stay in bed for a week to recover from her ordeal. She couldn't remember anything that happened between the time she fell into her coma until the time she found herself crawling through the snow toward the kitchen door with a throbbing hand. Which was probably a blessing.

We had the butler buried in the local graveyard. I didn't know whether to curse him or thank him. Papa routinely did both. But there's no doubt that if it weren't for him, Mama would not be with us today. So on balance, I think it was worth it.

32

Lords of the Manor

ST. CHARLES

Aunt Sukey only called upon the Lords of the Manor at the dark of the moon, never before nor after. She would walk down to the place where two roads met and would stand with a small staff, chanting softly in a strange tongue that I did not recognize, casting the important spells or calling upon the Lords of the Manor for advice or strength. I would creep from my bed to watch her sometimes. I'm sure she knew that I did, but she never objected. Unlike the mystical pow-wow doctors of the Pennsylvania Dutch tradition to the north, in which magical knowledge can only be passed between male and female relatives, the ability to work hoodoo magic could be passed along to anyone Aunt Sukey chose. And I was beginning to suspect that Aunt Sukey had chosen me—Dalila, her sister's daughter—as her successor.

I suppose that here in America, Aunt Sukey would be called a conjurer. But back home in Africa, she was known as a Waganga—a witch doctor—and a princess. Aunt Sukey called upon the Lords of the Manor to heal the sick, curse the wicked, and spare the lives of those who had been hexed by others. All of the slaves on our plantation held her in awe, and she arbitrated problems that arose, healed our sick, delivered babies, and often acted as emissary between us and the Master, who was a decent man, all things considered.

Aunt Sukey had a familiar spirit named Parti-gee-ho who walked with her wherever she went, though none of us regular folk could see it. Aunt Sukey said that Parti-gee-ho had the body of a great black ox, with cloven hooves, horns, a long tail, and huge nostrils that breathed fire and smoke. Its eyes were like live coals that burned the air around them. If we did anything to upset Aunt Sukey, we would hear some invisible *thing* snorting and stomping irritably. Then the miscreant would be sent flying into the air as if he or she had been kicked by an unseen creature. We children were all scared to death of Parti-gee-ho and would do whatever Aunt Sukey said rather than face her angry familiar.

My little brother—Sadiki—claimed he saw Parti-gee-ho's shadow once when he crept up to the open window of Aunt Sukey's cottage late one night. He saw her holding a long lock of blond hair that looked like it came from the head of the Master's wife, a cruel woman who often beat the slaves working in the house with a horse whip. Aunt Sukey dipped the lock of hair into a pile of salt and then into a pile of pepper arranged in rough wooden bowls on the table.

Sadiki didn't see what she did with the hair next, because at that moment, his eye was caught by a large, dark shadow that moved independently of Aunt Sukey and the flickering candles. It was huge and broad—the size of an ox—with sharp-looking horns and a flicking tail. Sadiki could see nothing at all in the place where the creature should have been standing in order to cast such a shadow, and this frightened him so much that he crept away from the window as silently as he could and then ran for home. A few days after Sadiki's visit to Aunt Sukey's cottage, the Master's wife took sick, and she died within a month.

It was shortly after her death that I was brought into the house to be a maid for the Master's eldest daughter, Miss Gracie. We were friends, Gracie and I, or as close to friends as you could be when you are owned by your friend's father. Miss Gracie was the one who taught me to read and write and speak like an educated white woman, rather than a poor black slave girl. But for all the educating she gave me, she could never shake my belief in the Lords of the Manor, which upset her quite a bit. Miss Gracie wanted me to be a good Christian, like she was, so I went to the chapel faithfully with the other slaves each Sunday. But I had seen too much of the powers that my people brought with them from the old world to scorn them in the new.

The day I turned thirteen, Aunt Sukey brought me down to her cottage after nightfall and began to teach me the secret ways of a Waganga. I learned to summon a reluctant person to me by blowing the contents out of an egg, inserting a lock of the person's hair into it so it protrudes at each end, and burying the egg in a path that person frequents. I learned that applying heartsease to a man's eyelids while he is sleeping will cause him to fall in love with the first woman he sees. I learned that placing dirt from the graveyard under a man's pillow will cause him to remain asleep until it is removed. And I learned many, many other things, too secret to be told. I also met Parti-gee-ho, who was everything Aunt Sukey had described and much more.

Most importantly, I learned to summon the Lords of the Manor. Some of them were dark, swirling creatures with long, thin hands and voices that hissed like serpents. They could be bound to you if you knew the right incantations and spells, or if you knew their names. Miss Gracie would have called them demons and would have dragged me to the minister to repent if she knew that I had any dealings with them. Some were creatures of incandescent light and shimmering brilliance. These beings could heal with a word or a touch, calm a frightened soul, and bring peace to a troubled mind. I think Miss Gracie would have called them angels. To me, dark or light, they were the Lords of the Manor and were to be treated with respect. Aunt Sukey taught me how to summon and deal with all of them, though I believe she primarily dealt with the ones made of light. She was a good woman and an excellent healer, and she was teaching me to be both so that I could carry on her work when she passed on.

Of course, there were the more mundane tasks associated with the craft, and Aunt Sukey taught me them all. I learned to make medicines from plants, herbs, powder of bones, seeds, roots, juices, leaves, and minerals. I found out all about healing treatments, including massage, thorns, bleeding, incantations, needles, ventriloquism, asking for sacrifice of a goat or chicken, or avoiding certain foods. And, of course, I learned to be a midwife. I had a gift for midwifery and soon found my services in demand far beyond my own plantation.

Much of the work of the Waganga resembled that of the white man's doctor. These were the parts I discussed with Miss Gracie, who thought I should go to medical school. Miss Gracie was a bit of a radical even then, and she believed in the rights of the individual, be they black or white, male or female. I knew, though she never told me, that she was saving up her money so that she could buy me from her father and set me free.

Well, the years passed swiftly—as they do—and one day a new young man came to our neighborhood, the youngest son of an English lord, and settled down to run his father's plantation. It was rumored among the plantation workers that young Henry had made things rather hot for himself in England, and his father had sent him to the States to get him out of some kind of difficulty.

I mentally labeled Henry a troublemaker and was very concerned when Miss Gracie came home one night a few months after her come-out ball with stars in her eyes and Henry's name on her lips. My heart sank, but I didn't say anything. I knew better than to argue with a woman so obviously in love.

I asked Aunt Sukey, who was by now very old (though still walking straight and tall, and still frightening children with stories of Parti-gee-ho) if there was some spell I could use to make a woman stop loving a man. Auntie's face grew grave, and she told me that this was wicked magic, and not to be thought of. When I explained about Miss Gracie, her countenance became solemn and still, but she still counseled against interfering in the relationship. Since she was the master and I the apprentice, I followed her instructions, albeit with a troubled heart.

Miss Gracie married Henry after a whirlwind courtship of only two months. I wept at her wedding, more from fear for my friend than joy at her happiness. She wanted me to come with her to Henry's plantation, but she did not insist when I stated a preference to remain among my own family and friends. In spite of her new interests and new love, Miss Gracie was still a radical, and she left the choice up to me rather than ordering me to go with her. I loved her all the more for treating me as an equal rather than a slave.

The first six months of the marriage sped past, and Miss Gracie glowed with happiness every time I saw her. It was not until she was expecting her first child that Henry's ardor began to cool, and the first sign of a serpent appeared in her paradise. Baby Harry was a year old when rumors of Henry's unfaithfulness reached my ears. I was betrothed now myself to a wonderful man, the grandson of one of Aunt Sukey's many acquaintances from the old world. Jacob had been raised on a neighboring plantation, and he'd earned his freedom in one go when he saved his Master's life during a terrible thunderstorm when the Master's horse spooked. I discussed the rumors with my Jacob, who confirmed that they were true. I thought again about the spell to make a woman stop loving a man, but I realized it was far too late to use it now. But my heart ached for Miss Gracie and her baby son.

On my wedding day, Miss Gracie came late to the church carrying little Harry. She had a black eye and a cut lip, which she had tried unsuccessfully to hide using white powder and rouge. She wept at my ceremony as I had wept at hers, but not—I think—for the same reasons. She never said a word about Henry, though we all knew that her injuries must have come from him. Henry had resumed the wild ways that had gotten him forcibly removed from England. His name was always paired now with that of some fast woman or another, and he was rapidly gambling away all the profits from his plantation. He was also a very cruel master, and many of his slaves ran away rather than suffer under his tyrannical rule. My Jacob heard later that Miss Gracie had received her black eye trying to defend one of the household slaves that her husband was beating.

By this time, Miss Gracie was expecting her second child. She came to visit her parents a month after my wedding, and I saw that she had grown thin and pale. She walked stiffly, as if her back and arms were too sore to move. I thought I saw the shadow of whip-marks through the thin material of her dress, but I could not be certain. She rested a hand tiredly on her round belly as she spoke with me, and her eyes brightened only when she looked at little Harry playing with some children by the pond.

A week later, my Jacob and I were getting ready for bed when we heard a desperate knocking at our door. It was pouring rain outside, with great peals of thunder and mighty flashes of lightning. We glanced at each other in puzzlement. Who could be out on such a night? Jacob wrenched open the door of our one-room cottage, and a soaking-wet, half-dead Miss Gracie stumbled inside, little Harry clutched in her bloodied arms. Her face was so swollen and bruised we could hardly recognize her, and her dress was torn and bloody where a whip had slashed again and again across her tender flesh. Jacob exclaimed in horror and caught Miss Gracie up in his strong arms. I gently detached the baby from her grasp. She clung to him for a moment with a desperate sob, and then she recognized me and let go in relief.

We put her into our bed and Jacob hastily strung up a rope and hung a blanket over it to give her some privacy while I tended her wounds. I could hear him singing softly to the frightened little boy as I tenderly washed out her cuts and soothed her bruised skin with my herbal remedies.

As I ministered to my friend, Miss Gracie gasped out the whole, terrible story, starting with Henry's unfaithfulness, his drunken rages, and the way he mistreated their slaves. But the climax had not come until earlier that evening, when Henry had brought home another woman and had asked Miss Gracie to move out of their bedroom so his lady-friend could sleep there in her place. When Miss Gracie had refused, he'd beaten her almost senseless and had threatened to beat little Harry too. As soon as he'd disappeared into his study with his vixen, she'd grabbed the baby and come running to us as fast as she could—stumbling through driving rain over mud-slicked roads, not daring to stop even to call for a carriage.

Miss Gracie was terrified that she might lose her unborn baby after the beating her husband had given her. As a trained midwife, I was able to ease her mind on that score. With her worst fear eased, Miss Gracie drifted off to sleep almost immediately.

I stared down at my dearest friend's bruised and battered but still lovely face, her blond locks scattered over the tattered pillow, and something inside me snapped. I didn't care if it was evil. I didn't care if my soul would be required of me for taking action. Henry had to be punished, and I was going to do it. What was the use of knowing how to call upon the Lords of the Manor if you couldn't use their power to right a most powerful wrong? I thrust aside the makeshift curtain and said curtly to Jacob: "Watch over Miss Gracie and the little one. I'm going out."

My new husband took one look at my grim face and asked no questions. Instead, he stood up, went to my workbench, and handed me the satchel in which I kept all the essential tools used by a Waganga. I gave him a nod, knowing that this was his way of saying he understood what I was going to do and supported my decision. Then I stalked out into the thunder and the pouring rain.

I was drenched to the skin almost at once, and my skirts clung heavily to my legs as I stalked through knee-deep mud along the lane toward the crossroads. By some happy coincidence—or perhaps fate—Henry had chosen the night of the new moon for his latest escapade, the most powerful night upon which to call the Lords of the Manor. My rage propelled me onward as I mulled over what I would do. I did not want anyone else in that ill-fated house to be hurt. I would need to warn them somehow.

I veered off the path and stopped at Aunt Sukey's cottage. I burst in with only the most preliminary knock, pulled her out of her bed, and told her to send a messenger in her name to the slaves on the next plantation. All of the slaves—even those that slept at the manor house—were to go immediately to the village and spend the night there. I knew such a command coming from Aunt Sukey, the Waganga for all the locals, would be obeyed at once. Aunt Sukey looked at me sharply. "What you going to do?" she asked gruffly, then shook her head. "Never you mind," she said. "I don't want to know."

She threw a shawl over my head as a protection against the downpour and ran across the yard to my brother Sadiki's house. Sadiki worked in the Master's stables, and there would be no questions asked if he borrowed a horse as long as he returned it by dawn. Satisfied, I continued toward the crossroads, rejoicing in the lightning and thunder and rain, for they had given me an idea.

I set my satchel on a wet, grassy place next to the road and took out the necessary ingredients for calling on the dark Lords of the Manor. When all was prepared, I stood at the very center of the crossroads and began to chant in the secret tongue taught to me by Aunt Sukey: "Come hither, my lord, my love, my dark one. Come hither and let down your midnight tresses."

The chant went on for one minute, then two. I felt prickles forming on my arms as the power grew. The wind began roaring through the tops of the trees, bringing with it dark, swirling creatures with long, thin hands and voices that hissed like a serpent. The sound of their coming was even louder than the thunder.

I called upon the Lords of the Manor who controlled the windstorms: the mighty cyclones, the monsoon, the tempest, and the whirlwind. I twisted slowly in place in the pouring rain, and the winds twisted with me, gaining power and speed as I whirled around and around, faster and faster. Then I released the winds with a gesture and watched as a mighty funnel stretched straight up into the sky. A perceptive observer, or one gifted with the Sight, might see—in addition to the twister—a great black ox, with cloven hooves, horns, a long tail, and huge nostrils that breathed fire and smoke. The creature rode the whirlwind sometimes before and sometimes aft, with a shadow darker than the night crouched on its back. Parti-gee-ho's red eyes burned the air around them as he bellowed his delight in the raging maelstrom surrounding him. He was answered by a cackle of agreement by the dark thing that rode him.

"Go thither, my lord, my love, my dark one, and do your work well," I murmured to Parti-gee-ho, and slowly tied the final pieces of the spell into the power of the crossroads and released the funnel to do its work. The whirlwind began marching its way toward the neighboring plantation, where Miss Gracie's husband drank with his lady-friend while his poor, beaten wife lay asleep in my humble cottage.

Sagging with weariness and the aftereffects of working a major spell, I gathered my things together and stumbled home to the makeshift bed my Jacob had made for us next to the hearth. I did not awaken until long past the dawn.

LORDS OF THE MANOR

Alarming reports had already spread through the village by the time I awoke. Henry's manor house and parts of his plantation had been razed to the ground by a huge tornado. Henry and his lady-friend, the only people in the house at the time, had been killed by the twister. Watchers from the village also reported seeing a Lord of the Manor astride a tall black ox riding the whirlwind, but this was discounted as superstition by our Master and Miss Gracie's stepmother, who were relieved beyond measure to find out that their daughter and grandson were safe.

After settling Miss Gracie and baby Harry into my friend's old rooms, I squared my shoulders and went down to see Aunt Sukey. She had forbidden me to summon the dark Lords of the Manor, and I had disobeyed her. Worse still, I was a murderess—though it could never be proved in a court of law. I considered my dark deed an execution, rather than a murder. Perhaps it was not my place to judge Henry, but who else would if not me? It was not considered a crime for a man to beat his wife and children, and short of killing Miss Gracie or Harry, Henry could probably wiggle out of any legal action taken against him, and go on to do it again. And Miss Gracie and her unborn child were too weak to live through another such beating.

I met Aunt Sukey coming up the path and stopped at once, lifting my chin and staring at her. As the master Waganga, she had the right to strip me of my rank and powers for disobeying her. I waited tensely to hear what punishment she would mete out, gazing into her dark, unfathomable eyes as squarely as I could. Then Aunt Sukey spoke: "Being a Waganga means making difficult choices. I did something similar once, for the same reason. Do not make it a habit."

With that, Aunt Sukey stalked passed me and on up to the manor house to deliver some of her home remedies to Miss Gracie. I felt my shoulders sag a bit as a weight dropped off my heart. And I remembered the Master's cruel first wife, who had died of a wasting disease shortly after my brother saw Aunt Sukey working a spell on her hair. I closed my eyes for a moment, overwhelmed by the memory, and by the weight and responsibility of my chosen profession. Then my Jacob's face flashed before my eyes, and I saw again the look he gave me as he handed me my satchel last night. I relaxed and slowly began walking down the familiar path to our cottage.

Next month, I thought, on the night of the new moon, I would go to the crossroads and summon the bright Lords of the Manor, those creatures of incandescent light and shimmering brilliance that could heal with a word or a touch. I would beg their forgiveness for my dark deed and ask for their guidance on my future path. Perhaps then I would be able to forgive myself. Perhaps.

33

The Werewolf's Bride

BALTIMORE

She was a high-spirited beauty who was the toast of the regiment, and he was a poor foot-soldier without two pennies to rub together. They would never have met at all, if the soldier had not chanced upon her one day while making his rounds. Her dress was caught by a briar bush, and she was endeavoring in vain to free herself. The soldier rushed to her aid. When he had freed her, the soldier gazed deeply into her sweet blue eyes as she thanked him prettily and lost his heart forever.

To his amazement, the soldier soon learned that his affections were returned. At the next town social, she would dance with no one but him; and she invited him to dinner to meet her parents. For a few days, there was some jealousy and sour faces among the men in his regiment, but their attitudes changed when the men observed the powerful love that had sprung up between the soldier and his lady.

Now the soldier's beautiful lady had caught the eye of an evil woodsman who had sold his soul to the devil in exchange for the ability to turn himself into a wolf at will. One evening, the woodsman lay in wait for the girl as she was walking home. He roughly accosted the soldier's lady, demanding that she elope with him. The maiden refused, spurning his love and crying loudly for someone to save her from his advances.

The girl's cries were heard by her fiancé, who had come searching when she was late returning to her parents' home. The soldier drove the woodsman away with harsh words, threatening him with dire consequences if he ever approached the maiden again.

The furious woodsman lay low for a few weeks, waiting for his chance. It came on the girl's wedding day. She was dancing happily at her wedding reception with a group of her friends when the woodsman, in the form of a wolf, leapt upon her and dragged her away with him.

The enraged bridegroom gave chase, but the wolf and the bride disappeared deep into the thick forest and were not seen again. For many days, the distraught soldier and his friends, armed with silver bullets that could kill a werewolf, scoured the woods in search of the maiden and her captor. Once the soldier thought he saw the wolf and shot at it. Upon reaching the location, he found a piece of a wolf's tail lying upon the ground, but there was no sign of the wolf to which it belonged.

After months of searching, the soldier's friends begged him to let the girl go and get on with living. But the soldier was half-mad with grief and refused to give up. And that very day, he found the remote bayside cabin where the werewolf lived. Within it lay the preserved body of his beloved wife. The girl had refused the werewolf's advances to the very end and had died for it.

When his murderous fury had faded away, the werewolf had tenderly laid the body of the girl he had loved and killed into

THE WEREWOLF'S BRIDE

a wooden coffin, where it would be safe from predators. The werewolf placed flowers on her coffin every day.

Lying in wait for his enemy, the soldier shot the werewolf several times as he entered the cabin. Maddened with pain, the werewolf fled, the soldier on his heels. With a howl of terror, the dying werewolf leapt into the bay and disappeared under the water.

The soldier sat by the bay, cradling his gun and waiting for the werewolf to surface so he could finish him off. But the water was still save for the little ripples blown by the wind. As the soldier watched, bloody pieces of the dead werewolf floated to the surface of the water and were consumed by the ever-present minnows.

When his friends from the regiment finally tracked him down, the soldier's mind was gone. He babbled insanely about a werewolf that had been eaten by a fish and sobered just long enough to lead the men to the body of his beloved. Then the soldier collapsed forevermore into insanity. He died a few days later and was buried beside his bride in a little glen where they had planned to build their house.

Their grave is long forgotten, and the place where it stands is covered with flowers in the spring. But to this day, the people of the area avoid the glen, though no one remembers why.

34

Don't Turn on the Light

PRINCE GEORGE'S COUNTY

She commandeered the small study room in the basement of her dormitory as soon as she realized she would have to pull an all-nighter in order to prepare for tomorrow's final exam in history. Her roommate, Jenna, liked to get to bed early, so she packed up everything she thought she would need and went downstairs to study . . . and study . . . and study some more.

Around midnight she ordered pizza and wings (thank goodness for all night cafés!) and munched away until close to two o'clock, when she realized that she'd left one of the textbooks she needed upstairs on her bed. She did a bit of creative cursing and for a moment contemplated leaving it there and just making do with the books she already had. But she knew that her professor had relied heavily on the information in that particular text in the midterm exam. With a dramatic sigh, she rose, stretched out the kinks in her back, and climbed the stairs slowly to her third-floor dorm room.

The lights were dim in the long hallway, and the old boards creaked under her weary tread. She'd have to walk more softly than that if she wasn't to wake Jenna, who was a light sleeper. She reached her room and turned the handle as softly as she could, pushing the door open just enough to slip inside, so that the hall lights wouldn't wake her roommate.

The room was filled with a strange, metallic smell that was new. She frowned a bit, her arms breaking out into chills. She was a bit frightened, though she could not fathom why. There was almost a feeling of malice in the room, as if a malevolent gaze were fixed upon her. Which was nonsense, of course. She obviously needed to get some sleep after finals were over, if this was the sort of trick her mind was starting to play on her.

She could hear Jenna breathing on the far side of the room—a heavy sound, almost as if she had been running. Jenna must have picked up a cold during the last tense week before finals. No wonder her roommate had wanted to go to bed early.

She crept along the wall until she reached her bed, groping among the covers for the stray history textbook. In the silence, she could hear a steady drip-drip-drip sound. She sighed silently. It must be the bathroom sink leaking again. Facilities had come to fix it just last week, but apparently they'd done a shoddy job. She'd have to call them again in the morning.

Her fingers closed on the textbook. She picked it up softly and withdrew from the room as silently as she could. There was no change in Jenna's heavy breathing, so she must not have awakened her. Good. Her roommate needed the rest to recover from her cold.

Relieved to be out of the room, she hurried back downstairs and collapsed into an overstuffed chair to peruse her book and take some more notes. The tedious hours ticked by. Around six o'clock, as it began to grow light outside, she decided that enough was enough. If she slipped upstairs now, she could get a couple hours' sleep before her nine o'clock exam. Collecting

DON'T TURN ON THE LIGHT

her books and papers, she packed up her bag and trudged slowly up the stairs to her room, exhausted almost beyond bearing.

The first of the sun's rays were beaming through the windows as she slowly slid the door open, hoping not to awaken Jenna. Her nose was met by an earthy, metallic smell a second before her eyes registered the scene in her dorm room. Jenna was spread-eagled on top of her bed against the far wall, her throat cut from ear to ear and her nightdress stained with blood. There was blood everywhere, spattered on the wall, saturating the bedclothes, and in a huge, congealing pool on the floor under the bed. As she gazed at the room in shock, two drops of blood fell from the saturated blanket with a drip-drip noise that sounded like a leaky faucet.

Vaguely, as if from a distance, she became aware of a horrible screeching sound. Scream after scream ripped through the building, as regular as clockwork. Dimly, she realized that she was the one wailing in terror, but she couldn't stop herself any more than she could cease wringing her hands. All along the hallway, she could hear voices exclaiming in fright, doors banging open, footsteps running down the passage.

Within moments, she was standing in the middle of a crowd in the doorway. Several other girls started to scream too, and people milled about in fright, exclaiming in horror at the scene before them. She felt her best friend—who stayed in a room a few doors down—grip her arm with a shaking hand. Her friend pointed a trembling finger toward the wall over her bed on the clean side of the room. She turned her head slowly to look, feeling old—very old.

Then her eyes widened in shock at what she saw on the wall. For a moment her heart seemed to stop in sheer terror. Then she fainted, hitting the floor with an audible thud.

On the wall above her bed, written in her roommate's blood, were the following words: "Aren't you glad you didn't turn on the light?"

Resources

"A Milk White Ghost. And the Consternation Which It Created on Shipboard." Cleveland, OH: *Cleveland Plain Dealer*, May 12, 1895.

"A True Ghost Story. The Mysterious White Horse That Appeared to a Maryland Parson." Jackson, MS: *Jackson Citizen*, December 12, 1882.

Asfar, Dan. *Haunted Battlefields.* Edmonton, AB: Ghost House Books, 2004.

Asfar, Dan and Thay, Edrick. *Ghost Stories of America.* Edmonton, AB: Ghost House Books, 2001.

———. *Ghost Stories of the Civil War.* Auburn, WA: Lone Pine Publishing, 2003.

Battle, Kemp P. *Great American Folklore.* New York: Doubleday & Company, Inc., 1986.

Blank, Trevor J. & Puglia, David J. *Maryland Legends: Folklore from the Old Line State.* Charleston, SC: The History Press, 2014.

Botkin, B. A., ed. *A Treasury of American Folklore.* New York: Crown, 1944.

———. *A Treasury of Southern Folklore.* New York: Crown Publishers, 1949.

Brewer, J. Mason. *American Negro Folklore.* Chicago, IL: Quadrangle Books, 1972.

Brown, Alan. *Stories from the Haunted South*. Jackson, MS: University Press of Mississippi, 2004.

Brunvand, Jan Harold. *The Choking Doberman and Other Urban Legends.* New York: W. W. Norton, 1984.

———. *The Vanishing Hitchhiker.* New York: W. W. Norton, 1981.

Carey, George G. *Maryland Folklore.* Centreville, MD: Tidewater Publishers, 1989.

———. *Maryland Folklore and Folklife.* Centreville, MD: Tidewater Publishers, 1970.

Coffin, Tristram. P., and Hennig Cohen, eds. *Folklore in America.* New York: Doubleday & AMP, 1966.

———. *Folklore from the Working Folk of America.* New York: Doubleday, 1973.

Cohen, Daniel. *Ghostly Tales of Love & Revenge.* New York: Putnam Publishing Group, 1992.

Cohen, Daniel, and Susan Cohen. *Hauntings & Horrors.* New York: Dutton Children's Books, 2002.

Coleman, Christopher K. *Ghosts and Haunts of the Civil War.* Nashville, TN: Rutledge Hill Press, 1999.

Crites, Susan. *Lively Ghosts Along the Potomac.* Martinsburg, WV: Butternut Publications, 1997.

Dahlgren, Madeleine Vinton. *South Mountain Magic: Tales of Old Maryland.* Maple Shade, NJ: Lethe Press, 2002.

Dorson, R. M. *America in Legend.* New York: Pantheon Books, 1973.

Editors of Life. *The Life Treasury of American Folklore*. New York: Time Inc., 1961.

Erdoes, Richard, and Alfonso Ortiz. *American Indian Myths and Legends*. New York: Pantheon Books, 1984.

Flanagan, J. T., and A. P. Hudson. *The American Folk Reader*. New York: A. S. Barnes & Co., 1958.

Gallagher, Trish. *Ghosts & Haunted Houses of Maryland*. Centreville, MD: Tidewater Publishers, 1988.

Godwin, David. *True Ghosts 2: More Haunting Tales from the Vaults of FATE Magazine*. Woodbury, MN: Llewellyn Publications, 2010.

Hauck, Dennis William. *Haunted Places: The National Directory*. New York: Penguin Books, 1994.

Holub, Joan. *The Haunted States of America*. New York: Aladdin Paperbacks, 2001. "John Wilkins, Sharpshooter." Washington, DC: *The Morning Times*, March 28, 1897.

Honigman, Andrew. *True Ghosts: Haunting Tales from the Vaults of FATE Magazine*. Woodbury, MN: Llewellyn Publications, 2012.

Lake, Matt. *Weird Maryland*. New York: Sterling Publishing Co., Inc., 2006.

Leach, M. *The Rainbow Book of American Folk Tales and Legends*. New York: The World Publishing Co., 1958.

Leeming, David, and Jake Page. *Myths, Legends, & Folktales of America*. New York: Oxford University Press, 1999.

Lewis, John. *Tales of the Eastern Shore*. Wilmington, DE: Cedar Tree Books, 1997.

Macken, Lynda Lee. *Haunted Baltimore: Charm City Spirits.* Forked River, NJ: Black Cat Press, 2004.

Mott, A. S. *Ghost Stories of America, Vol. II.* Edmonton, AB: Ghost House Books, 2003.

Mumma, Wilmer McKendree. *Ghosts of Antietam.* Self-published, 1996.

Okonowicz, Ed. *The Big Book of Maryland Ghost Stories.* Mechanicsburg, PA: Stackpole Books, 2010.

———. *Haunted Maryland.* Mechanicsburg, PA: Stackpole Books, 2007.

———. *In the Vestibule.* Elkton, MD: Myst and Lace Publishers, Inc., 1994.

———. *Pulling Back the Curtain, Vol. I.* Elkton, MD: Myst and Lace Publishers, Inc., 1994.

———. *Terrifying Tales of Beaches and Bays.* Elkton, MD: Myst and Lace Publishers, Inc., 2001.

Peck, Catherine, ed. *A Treasury of North American Folk Tales.* New York: W. W. Norton, 1998.

Polley, J., ed. *American Folklore and Legend.* New York: Reader's Digest Association, 1978.

Reevy, Tony. *Ghost Train!* Lynchburg, Va.: TLC Publishing, 1998.

Roberts, Nancy. *Civil War Ghost Stories & Legends.* Columbia, SC: University of South Carolina Press, 1992.

_____. *The Haunted South.* Columbia, SC: University of South Carolina Press, 1988.

Schwartz, Alvin. *Scary Stories to Tell in the Dark.* New York: Harper Collins, 1981.

Skinner, Charles M. *American Myths and Legends*, Vol. 1. Philadelphia: J. B. Lippincott, 1903.

———. *Myths and Legends of Our Own Land*, Vol. 2. Philadelphia: J. B. Lippincott, 1896.

Spence, Lewis. *North American Indians: Myths and Legends Series.* London: Bracken Books, 1985.

Thay, Edrick. 2003. *Ghost Stories of the Old South.* Auburn, WA: Ghost House Books.

Zeitlin, Steven J., Amy J. Kotkin, and Holly Cutting Baker. *A Celebration of American Family Folklore.* New York: Pantheon Books, 1982.

About the Author

S. E. Schlosser has been telling stories since she was a child, when games of "let's pretend" quickly built themselves into full-length tales acted out with friends. A graduate of Houghton College, the Institute of Children's Literature, and Rutgers University, she created and maintains the award-winning website Americanfolklore.net, where she shares a wealth of stories from all fifty states, some dating back to the origins of America. Sandy spends much of her time answering questions from visitors to the site. Many of her favorite e-mails come from other folklorists who delight in practicing the old tradition of who can tell the tallest tale.

About the Illustrator

Artist **Paul Hoffman** trained in painting and printmaking. His first extensive illustration work was on assignment in Egypt, drawing ancient wall reliefs for the University of Chicago. His work graces books of many genres: children's titles, textbooks, short story collections, natural history volumes, and numerous cookbooks. For *Spooky Maryland*, he employed a scratchboard technique and an active imagination.

CPSIA information can be obtained
at www.ICGtesting.com
Printed in the USA
LVHW031924130521
687356LV00007B/874